A GUIDE TO CREATIVE BUREAUCRACY:

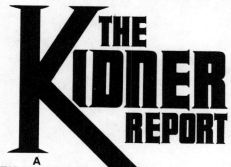

THE KIDNER REPORT

A
SATIRICAL LOOK
AT
BUREAUCRACY
AT THE
PAPER CLIP
AND
STAPLER LEVEL

"Classified material will be considered lost when it cannot be found."

—U.S. Navy Security Instruction

A GUIDE TO CREATIVE BUREAUCRACY:

THE KIDNER REPORT

A SATIRICAL LOOK AT BUREAUCRACY AT THE PAPER CLIP AND STAPLER LEVEL

JOHN KIDNER

acropolis

Published by ACROPOLIS BOOKS LTD. ● WASHINGTON, D.C. 20009

ACROPOLIS BOOKS LTD.
Colortone Building, 2400 17th St., N.W.
Washington, D.C. 20009

Printed in the United States of America by
COLORTONE PRESS Creative Graphics Inc., *Washington, D. C. 20009*

Library of Congress Cataloging in Publication Data

Kidner, John, 1923-
  The Kidner report.

  At head of title: A guide to creative bureaucracy.
  1. Bureaucracy--Anecdotes, facetiae, satire, etc.
I. Title. II. Title: A guide to creative bureaucracy.
JF1601.K5   301.18'32'0207   72-3814
ISBN 0-87491-337-3
ISBN 0-87491-338-1 (pbk)

DEDICATION

To my wife, Christine, and my son, John Craig, neither of whom took kindly to my Bureaucratic responses when they asked for: (1) household money, (2) the car, (3) allowances, (4) explanations of where I had been.

CONTENTS

Page

Prologue 7

1 B-Day 9

2 The Spectre of Negativism 14

3 The Sons of Bureaucracy (SOB)
and Their Basic Drives 18

4 "The Old Bureaucratic System (BS)" 25

5 The Program Cycle 33

6 The Protective Vocabulary 42

7 To Build a Proclamation 54

8 The Universal Response (UR) 59

9 The Principal of Amorphism 61

10 The Protective Vocabulary:
Generalized Proper and Non-Proper
Utilization 66

11 Explaining Things 70

12 Studies 76

13 Reports 79

14 Formsmanship 82

15 The Paper Criterion 85

16 The Sea of Coordination 92

17 Abuses 101

18 The Lance and Windmill Syndrome 104

19 Money of Unspecified Denomination (MUD) . 107

20 "I Don't Know" 110

21 "I.I.D.I.F.Y.I.G.T.D.I.F.E." **116**

22 Delusion Depths
(Part 1 of a Trilogy on Accolades) **119**

23 Medals and Citations: Another Path to the
River (Part 2 of a Trilogy on Accolades) . **122**

24 The Power of Suggestion
(Part 3 of a Trilogy on Accolades) **126**

25 Ritual of Presentation (ROP) **129**

26 To Err Is Bureaucracy, Too **133**

27 Overtiming **137**

28 Manpower Reductions and
Protective Reorganizations **142**

29 Walls **145**

30 Gatherings of Bureaucrats **149**

31 Clerkdom **157**

32 Etc. **161**

Epilogue **163**

Glossary **164**

PROLOGUE

ENTERING WASHINGTON, D.C. via the Memorial Bridge—
busses and protest marchers permitting—one catches an arrest-
ing glimpse of the Lincoln Memorial, the Capitol dome, and the
Washington Monument. These and the mighty fortress of huge
government office buildings—their window-punched, flat sides
looking like IBM cards—remind the beholder that this is the
world's last bastion of productive democracy and the first
bastion of Bureaucracy, Washington's other monument.

But all this hallowed stone can't obscure the colossal,
bronze equestrian statues standing one on each side of the
bridge's D.C. terminus. And it doesn't take long, either, to
realize that even as these great horses face the city, their massive
behinds address the Nation!

"Well," say some, "Washington's always behind anyway,
so that's the first thing someone should see. They *ought* to
stand that way!"

Others whisper of subconscious forces at work—hidden things . . . attitudes, perhaps . . . that made the statues' positioning a Freudian slip. Still others swear that after a long, fruitless study by an ad hoc committee, the orientation was determined by tossing a coin, and that since Bureaucracy never gets the tail end of anything, the outcome was historically consistent.

Characteristically, though, the real truth lies buried under great piles of misunderstanding. It seems that one day the planning committee chairman was asked by his secretary, "What's your wife's middle name, sir," at the same time the foreman in charge of erecting the statues stuck his head in the door and asked, "Which way you want their tails, Mac." The harried official answered his secretary saying, "Virginia," and the foreman, of course, went back to the statues thinking the answer was the sovereign state across the river . . . etc. . . . etc.

And now they stand, a fortuitous monument to the misunderstandings that so often provoke the insult symbolized in their mighty haunches.

Named *Valor* and *Sacrifice* now, perhaps some new age—a more enlightened one—will honor the weeping need that Bureaucracy has for *understanding* and *forbearance,* and after turning the horses around, will rename them accordingly.

1

B-DAY!

BY 13 NOVEMBER 1982, everybody in the United States will be employed by government. Department of Labor statistics bless this conclusion with validity and make it more comfortable to accept. Specifically, the latest *Manpower Report for the President* shows that in 1965 the population was 194.6 million, and that 19.3 million were People Employed Because Government Buys Goods and Services (PEBGBGAS). This ten-to-one ratio dropped in two years to 8.7 to one, then by 1969 to 8.3 to one. Plotted on paper with the trend line extended until it crosses the "everybody line"—the one-to-one point—we see that 13 November 1982 is Bureaucracy Day! B-Day! Everybody a government employee—*a capital letter Bureaucrat!*

B-day!
Everybody a government employee—
a capital letter Bureaucrat

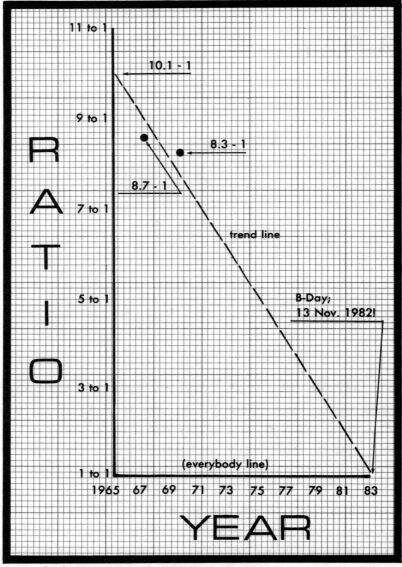

Dept. of Labor, March 1970, table G-7, page 327.

Unfortunately for the unacquainted, the thought of a whole nation full of Bureaucrats is as grim as granite. This is attributable to a slanted credo of the outside world which says:

a. People who work for the government sit around and shuffle papers; they don't have to be productive to keep their jobs.

b. Working for the government stifles initiative and discourages independence.

c. Bureaucrats are generally unhygienic and of illegitimate birth.

However, once more some solid facts will help demonstrate the error of such a credo.

Take "a" for example. In 1968-69 the Gross National Product (GNP) increased by $66.4 billion, and at the same time the number of PEBGBGAS went up by 400,000. Some crude division reveals that for every new Bureaucrat added, the GNP jumped by $166,000! This is a government employee level of productivity unequaled anywhere in the world!

Point "b" of the credo crumbles just as easily. Not all PEBGBGAS work *directly* in federal, state and local government. In fact, in 1965 only 10.0 million out of a workforce of 71 million did so. This means that there was one government employee looking out for six who worked elsewhere. By 1969 the number dropped to five, thus for each five years that pass, any given employee has one less person to take care of. At this rate, in 25 years it will be every man for himself! Total independence! And all this because Bureaucracy has the initiative to find others to help with the work.

Point "c" falls the easiest. Consider that most of Bureaucracy's jobs are white collar and carried on in bright, antiseptic offices. Moreover, from Department of Health, Education, and Welfare statistics we learn that currently there are about 1.6

million illegitimates of working age. So even if every last one were employed by government, there would be only one illegitimate for each 12 employees, and he would be clean. Put more bluntly, there are not nearly as many dirty bastards working for the government as people say there are.

There's a great deal of resistance to be overcome if the B-Day legions entering the Corridors of Bureaucracy (COB) are to check their shoulder chips at the door. Admittedly, the foregoing are small arguments for clearing up the misunderstanding. So I offer this manual as a bulldozer to help do the job. It explains most of the hows and whys of good Bureaucratting at the paper clip and stapler level, and does so in much the same way a book on magic might take the mystery out of the impossible escape trick. Hopefully, the effect will be the same: the awe will be gone once the secret's simplicity is exposed. One should then feel like saying, "It's so *obvious* now!" Thus let in on it, the hostility that greets the strange and unknown will evaporate and let some understanding in.

The lessons are written with three categories of students in mind, all of whom have one thing in common. In their encounters with Bureaucracy they learn by trial and error and error and error.

Primarily, it is the young man who is just beginning his career as a Bureaucrat—the novice, the *tyrocrat*—as opposed to the practicing, experienced *maestrocrat,* who will benefit most. However, Bureaucrats still in the embryo stage despite all their years in the Agencies will find it helpful, too. So also will the people who still cling to the outside world's "This seems to be a reasonable approach."

Finally, there are the Outside World People (OWP), each of whom from time to time has hurled himself against Bureaucracy's bulwarks in a futile rage over what he believes are acts of regimented stupidity.

In a word then, this book is written for the enlightenment of those who work or will work in Bureaucracy as well as for the OWPs who may feel worked by it. Grasped and applied, the material presented should make B-Day a joyful one, much anticipated for the complete orderliness that will arrive with it.

Most will find the text a Welcome and Timely Treatise (WATT); others, no doubt, will see it as no more than a lot of Canards, Revelations, Accusations and Pronouncements. In any case, accepted in the context of its ultimate purpose, it is a modest start toward turning *Valor* and *Sacrifice* around.

2

THE SPECTRE OF
NEGATIVISM

WHEN BUREAUCRACY EXACTS the last full measure of compliance, it is often mistaken for a Negative Attitude. This particular misunderstanding is the penalty paid for dedication to consistency and equal treatment under the Bureaus, and clearly, there are a number of martyrs to it.

A health department official in Satellite Beach, Florida, for example, closed down an 11-year-old boy's sidewalk lemonade stand because it had no restroom facilities. In doing so, officials explained, "We're just trying to protect the health of the public. We're not picking on little boys."

An Internal Revenue employee was kidnapped as he was making an official collection call, and was forced at gunpoint to drive his abductor several hundred miles from the scene. Escaping uninjured he returned next day and promptly filed a claim for mileage. "The trip was made on government time," he explained. Nevertheless, payment was refused on the grounds that there was really no connection between the call and the kidnapping "except that he was on official business at or near the place where the abduction took place." Regulations defined reimbursable costs as only those "confined to expenses essential to the transacting of official business."

In Newcastle-Upon-Tyne, England, a demolition crew was razing homes to make way for new construction. Among them was the house of Arthur Whitby. However, nowhere in the city's records was there any reference to show that such a house existed. So when the wrecking crew appeared for work, they were turned away because they lacked the proper permits. The bewildered workmen appealed to the city council who ruled that the fact the men had just come from the house was not germaine. "There is no official record of such a house," they elaborated, "and how can you tear something down that just isn't there?"

Another case involved Federal statutes which forbid importing contraceptives. A customs official enforced the ban with marked thoroughness by ordering a young Swedish lady to throw her diaphragm into New York harbor, before admitting her past the barriers.

They were equally as consistent when a New York couple tried to bring in a 70-year old slot machine purchased in England for $18.12. It was of French make and worked only with French coins of the era. But it was a gambling device so it was confiscated. Later it was sent to the Smithsonian Institution.

Finally there was the case of an invalid mother of two who was evicted because her welfare check didn't arrive in time to pay the rent. An inquiry revealed that regulations prohibited checks being sent out until the case medical records were in, and the lady's had not been received. Then, the check couldn't be written because other instructions required this to be done with a check-writing machine which was not available because it was some other office's turn to use it. When the rent check did come, the lady was already hanging the curtains in her new home in a neighbor's cellar.

No doubt these stories have awakened your ire, and at first one sides with the young boy, the Swedish lady, the evicted mother and the others. But this is not unusual because, under the influence of misunderstanding, even the most sage can be led to a wrong conclusion by the correct route just as easily as they can be led to the right conclusion by an erroneous route.

For instance, some ad hoc biologists experimented with fleas. They put a specimen in a large glass jar and struck the side, producing a loud reverberating ring. The startled flea jumped 18 inches, which was recorded. Then two of its legs were removed and the jar struck again. This time the flea jumped only nine inches. Two more legs were removed and he jumped three inches. At last all the legs were removed and despite repeated strikes, the flea didn't budge. The scientists concluded that fleas without legs can't hear.

In all these cases, the really dedicated Bureaucrat was the victim. Charities, men of the cloth, neighbors, civic groups, and semi-official busybodies may form coalitions to force Bureaucracy to ignore, for a few, the regulations written for the benefit of the many. But Bureaucracy usually succeeds in holding out to the end. The Bureaucrats who man the ramparts become martyrs indeed, having suffered a roasting by the media for doing no more than a good job of knowing and enforcing the rules.

Throughout these characteristic enforcements, Bureaucracy performs according to the character stresses within the Bureaucrats themselves, and the SYSTEM through which the stresses are relieved. Unfortunately, negativism arises out of the process like the aroma from strong cheese, and similarly, belies the wholesome goodness that gives it life.

So this text must begin with an explanation of the Spectre of Negativism in hope that it can be exorcised. This will help put the lessons to come in a more positive light, and in turn, may prove that Bureaucracy's true character is not made up of "NO!!" and "WE CAN'T DO THAT."

3

THE SONS OF BUREAUCRACY (SOB) AND THEIR BASIC DRIVES

THIS PART OF the text attempts to define the unique qualities that mark the Bureaucrat apart from all others. These, however, prove too elusive. Yet to dispel the dread spectre, these traits must be laid out where people can see them. Thinking that my fellowcrats, like myself, were too far on the inside to recognize the qualities, I turned to the outside world. Approaching an acquaintance who was a profit taker in the classic sense, I explained about the book and my problem and concluded by asking, "What do you think the prime requisites of a good Bureaucrat are?"

His reply—"Gray hair for the look of distinction, and hemorrhoids for the look of concern."—led me to believe immediately that he and the others like him may not be in sympathy with the task I'd set for myself.

Shaken, I hurried back to the familiar, comfortable cubicles of the Agencies, determined to define the characteristic stresses myself, and to hell with the outside world.

Then one day the main stress was defined for me.

My wife, who is confined to a wheel chair, has to have a companion and housekeeper with her constantly. So she hired Marie, a large, serious, hard-working woman of about 55. One afternoon, in preparation for a small informal dinner, Marie was asked to polish the silverware. After a couple of quiet hours of rubbing and humming, she proudly laid the utensils out in a gleaming line for my wife to admire, pointing out that, "One of the spoons was bent a little bit, ma'am. But I fixed it." Only a glance was required for my wife to see that the once deep, graceful arc of the gravy ladle now conformed nicely to the more gentle curve of all the other spoons! It was a slightly wavy curve but a fine approximation, considering that Marie had used no special tools.

Therein lies the vital trait exposed and unashamed. Born Bureaucrats must *want things to conform to an established pattern enough to force a fit when they do not.*

Take, for example, the case of a young secretary who was summoned by the New York City authorities to pay a parking ticket put on her car a few days after it had been stolen. Missing the point completely, she complained that she shouldn't have to pay the fine. "After all, I wasn't in charge of the car. The thief was," she exclaimed. She came close to showing that she understood, though, when she asked why the police could find the car to put a ticket on it, but could not find it to recover it.

Bureaucracy's penchant for reshaping any gravy ladle that may need polishing presupposes a set of standards. Somebody had to put that curve in the other spoons in the first place. This honor goes to those who originally conceive the procedures and programs that establish the conformity guides through which the unconforming are brought into the System. To them go the elevators to the carpeted floors and impressive desks; everybody else must take the stairs.

The rapidity of rise and the heights attained depend upon the way the conformity is achieved. Marie, who would have all the spoon handles curve exactly the same, exercised the most expedient but least imaginative option. She could have taken a grander course and reshaped all the other spoons to fit the ladle! Or she could have done the spectacular and reshaped all of them to a new curve entirely!

The decision making that looms implicit in these options may be a little frightening at first. But on-the-job training (OJT) and some experience will cause the right decision to fall into place almost automatically. For example, some time ago the Smithsonian Institution acquired a 300 foot by 60 foot room to be used as an addition to the Fine Arts Portrait Gallery. The space had previously been occupied by Bureaucrats from "the old Patent Office." The huge room had 32 columns and pilasters, and four lintels all of exquisite marble. However, exquisite marble was not called for in the procedures establishing patent office decor, and conformity was achieved by five coats of government-green paint. Clearly, this was a case of merely straightening the gravy ladle.

Another case is one wherein the Executive Branch of Government complained bitterly because the Federal agencies were generating and storing too much paper. This embarrassment of riches was temporarily disposed of by directing that no more filing cabinets would be purchased. Here, the other spoons were reshaped to fit the ladle.

Finally, there was the problem of gold flow in Vietnam. In 1966 American soldiers were converting greenbacks into piasters at such a rate that impossible inflationary pressures were being put on the native currency. The dollar influx had to be stopped. After a couple of false starts (high interests rates to induce savings; putting notorious piaster sumps off-limits), General Westmoreland launched "Operation MOOSE—Move Everybody Out of Saigon Earliest." Shortly thereafter, thousands of Americans who'd previously paid rent in the teaming city were living on government reservations in the nearby suburbs. But after all these spoons were configured to a new shape entirely, as it were, work began on the problem of how to discourage the Americans from spending like tourists instead of residents, when they went to town in the evenings.

No matter that the conformity urge is deeply ingrained. Sometimes there are pressures to ignore it, and weak Bureaucrats often succumb. This is probably due to a very human desire on their part to:

a. Get the small jobs out of the way so they can leave early.

b. Help somebody else who is in a hurry, or is being pressured.

c. Clean up the loose ends before going on a trip.

d. Get the paperwork caught up with the circumstances.

e. Meet the latest extended deadline.

f. Get on to something a lot more interesting.

To ignore the conformity urge may seem a small thing, and a wholly forgivable one. But this always requires making an *exception,* i.e., doing a *non-conformity.* As a result, a fellowcrat will be bypassed, a regulation broken, details overlooked, and the whole thing forced *out of pattern* so that everybody can see and criticize it. This is why, in Bureaucracy, quick work is never mistaken for efficiency.

For example: the town of Groesbeck, Texas, wanted to

pave some of the major streets and asked that the Federal Government help pay for the work done in front of the Post Office. They took a short cut by asking that a little paving, and nothing more, be considered. "The government's share is only $250," boasted the city fathers. Fortunately a conscientious Bureaucrat recognized that nothing could be done for $250, and assumed the figure to be the product of a non-conformity, brought on by not following the procedures for paving streets in front of Post Offices. After the facts were explained, the estimate was resubmitted at $60,000 which included charges for a little sewer work, too. This conformed, nobody was hurt, and the funds were approved at once.

There is a second basic counterforce to the conformity urge and it is so strong that even the best of us are often forced to yield. This is *the need to be hailed as a "good ole boy" (GOB)*.

Indeed, one does not walk the Agency halls very long before he hears an off-the-cuff character analysis concluded with "Yessir. He's a good ole boy." This is among the highest unofficial accolades possible, and to earn it the Bureaucrats must:

a. Conform to the Programs written by fellowcrats, without complaining too much or asking for exceptions too often.

b. Keep from offending anybody in particular by refraining from officially or directly disagreeing with another's proposals, and/or agreeing with others when they express the opinion that "those people" don't know what they're doing.

c. Stay busy without making extra work for somebody else.

d. Avoid being blunt when saying officially what must be said about the quality and quantity of a fellowcrat's work, his ability, IQ, or initiative.

e. Understand regulations well enough to find a loophole

which will help a fellowcrat who approaches with the right attitude.

f. Avoid being too right too often.

The need to be a Good Ole Boy evolved out of the leisurely post-World War II era when people were fed up with "You will . . . " but would respond to "Would you please . . . ?" Today, reaching full GOB status requires that Bureaucrats always deal with each other with Sympathy, Neighborliness, Objectivity, Willingness, Joviality, Open-mindedness, and Benignity.

There is an interesting sidelight here. In officialdom one often hears the expression "snow job"; i.e., "It sure sounds like a snow job to me." Used thus, it implies that an opinion, excuse, reason, or explanation has been couched in terms that are deliberately confusing, or designed to be so complimentary as to be placating, or both. Originally, though, the meaning was found in the acronym derived from the GOB characteristics just listed. Back then it was one word, "SNOWJOB" and was applied to a fellowcrat who had used all the GOB traits with exceptional skill. For instance, "Boy! Jack sure gave the inspectors a SNOWJOB."

The concessions that conformity makes to the Good Ole Boy syndrome are responsible for the System having to bump along over a series of compromises. The results, however, are almost always adequate, but are termed *excellent* if they close the gap between what actually happens and what should happen. They are termed *superior* if they prevent what is expected to happen from happening before the paperwork is complete.

Conformity and the GOB syndrome ultimately unite in a System which binds Bureaucracy in a common effort, thus making it the same whether epitomized in Washington, at the city clerk's office, or in any large business. It's true there may be isolated cases of just plain cussedness here and there, but there is no such thing as a deliberately Negative Attitude. Rather, the Spectre of Negativism turns out to be no more than the outward manifestation of an inward turmoil. Torn between the GOB need to be loved and the need for things to conform, the Bureaucrat must say "yes" in such a way that he pays homage to both drives. It is this that so often makes the "yes" come out sounding a good bit like "no."

4

"THE OLD BUREAUCRATIC SYSTEM (BS)"

HISTORICALLY, the urge to have things conform to categories and to be disposed of automatically comes to rest as a system of some sort. Bureaucracy as the ultimate in conformity produced *The System,* the ultimate in organized processing techniques (OPT). It has been around in one form or another ever since man first learned that people would be more apt to do something if the request were put in writing and followed a format. Because of its birth in antiquity it is affectionately called "The Old Bureaucratic System" or just "The ole BS."

All organizations use some kind of system, but Bureaucracy's stands out by virtue of its sheer size and inertia. In my tyrocrat days, each attempt to use it was like moving a king-size mattress with the carry grips torn off. But my irritation over so much system waned after trying out those used in credit card billing, or getting a magazine change of address processed. It died out completely, however, when I realized that with so many people doing things, and so many done for, Bureaucracy just had to be big and different.

One notes, for example, that Bureaucracy functions through a series of *Programs*. These, in turn, are made up of *Projects* which themselves are comprised of *Tasks* which fellow-crats *strive* to *finalize*. Two or more tasks in combination become an *Effort*. Thus, "We have three more tasks to do on the F-one-eleven effort before all the program's projects are finalized."

This particular hernia-giving terminology (Herniology, I prefer to call it) is the System's way of directing attention to the corded muscles and teeth-gritting labor that is so common to it. It distinguishes Bureaucracy from the outside world where people merely *work* at doing *jobs*.

The System is actually a way of life where decisions are approached, in writing, step by measured step, probed and tested with all the conscientiousness of a barefoot coolie in a field full of briars. Results are ground out at an unhurried pace, thus reassuring everyone that any problem, plan, proposal, or ‚plea—irrespective of cost or size—will receive exactly the same consideration. This is the *Principle of Equal Treatment (PET)*, and, incidentally, the origin of the expression, "PET Project."

The Principle is upheld by seeing to it that each case to be striven over is stripped of its apparent simplicity and rearranged into the complexity it really is—or should be.

Examples are endless and classics are not hard to find. In 1961, for example, the Defense Supply Agency began consider-ing a black-finish belt buckle that would be standard for all the services. In that same year the first firm plans were made for landing a man on the moon. The belt buckle was a 35 cent item; the moon trip was a billion dollar effort. Nonetheless, eight years later when Neil Armstrong took his one small step, the belt buckle decision was (and as yet, still is) pending.

Sometimes comprehending this much Bureaucracy is easier when comparing it to a computer. These, the absolute zenith of automated paper handling, can hold the spectator spellbound with their flashing lights, banks of switches, whirling tapes, the blur of riffling cards dropping neatly into the respective compartments just waiting to receive them and their awesome results in the form of great stacks of paper. A favorite way of introducing the novice to one of them is to invite him to play a game with it, say, tic-tac-toe. Futile though he knows it to be, he grins sheepishly and timidly picks up the gauntlet. Within a click and a switch throw, the computer wins, then good naturedly it softens the blow with some facetious comment—

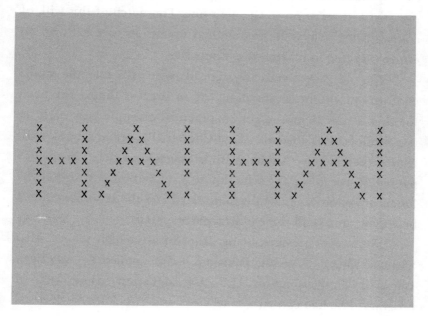

Invariably, the loser responds with an admiring "Gosh! It's almost human!" This is the desired reaction for it sets up the astounded stranger to be reassured by, "Yeah. But don't forget. It's gotta be programmed. It won't do a damned thing unless somebody tells it exactly what to do, and when and how to do it."

Continuing the analogy, each step the machine goes through is very carefully spelled out in advance. The instructions include a description of the circumstances that must be present to trigger a process step, cues by which each component will add its bit, addresses so it will drop its punch-cards in the right slot, and something to tell it to stop. The unique language used, the need for even the most elementary step to be written out in full detail, and the capacity for endless search and repetition, are responsible for the computer's success in automatic problem solving. The only thing it asks is that the inputs be exactly right. If not, it will choke, bog down for a while, reject the misfit, then go on to the next one. Too much of this will, of course, bring any well-programmed operation to a halt. So no effort is spared in making the inputs fit.

The old Bureaucratic System likewise asks that the inputs conform to the programs designed to process them. The need for this is now being taught by practical example very early in our schools. For instance, at a Chester, Pa. grade school, officials suspended two students for bringing sandwiches instead of paying 35 cents for the school lunches. The reason was that the lunch program was federally subsidized and the school wouldn't be eligible unless all the children participated.

Nor are the lessons being dropped after high school. Miss Sultana Ismail, a young Pakistani lady, applied to American University in Washington, D.C., for admission to the doctoral program. She had earned a Bachelors and two Masters degrees, each from universities in the United States, and had lived in the States for a number of years. Nonetheless, the admission clerk insisted she take an English language proficiency test, because "It is required for all foreign students. And besides, it's been over five years since the last time you took it, and that's all they allow."

The System has a unique problem because one office's output is another office's input. Since there are millions of offices in Bureaucracy, there are millions of inputs being striven over every day. Most of this striving goes into writing instructions, for only by means of the most detailed "hows" and "whens" can Bureaucracy, like the computer, cue its components to chime in with their thing at exactly the right time. One may, then, look upon a Program as the complete body of instructions on a given subject, coupled with the historical accounts of how they were carried out, i.e., adhered to.

The Program's instructions can be an elementary statement. For instance, a placard in the hallway of the Frankfort, Germany, bachelor officers' quarters tells the occupants: IN CASE OF FIRE, STAND IN THE HALL AND SHOUT 'FIRE!'

Instructions become more complex as the subjects get more complicated. For example, a U.S. Treasury publication on Pursuit Driving warns: "If there is a choice of hitting a fixed object at 40 miles per hour or more, or rolling the car, a roll is better. A car will roll over if the driver jerks the wheel abruptly, and at the same time, floors both pedals. It is best to reduce speed sufficiently in braking so that you may miss the object and still remain upright with a degree of control."

Equally complex is this 1965 instruction from Federal Regulations on private flying: "An applicant for a private pilot certificate (airplane) must hold a student pilot certificate endorsed for solo and cross-country flights and must have had . . . at least 20 hours of solo flight time of which at least 15 were in an airplane."

More heavily involved issues are typified by the following memo prepared by a conscientious Bureaucrat for then-Secretary of the Treasury Fowler to sign:

To All Personnel of the Treasury Department
Subject: Falls Prevention Campaign, 1967

This is to request your assistance in a very important campaign to be conducted throughout the Treasury Department during 1967—the prevention of injuries to employees as a result of falls. More Treasury employees percentage-wise are injured by falls than in any other Federal agency except two rather small ones. This has been a serious problem for ten years and deserves the serious consideration of all personnel, because all of us are potential victims of serious injuries.

The prevention of falls will not be easy. They result when people fall over objects, out of chairs, down steps and stairs, and even over their own feet. Some can be traced to hazards; others would appear to result from plain carelessness and inattention.

I have called on the Heads of Bureaus to take steps to institute effective inspection and clean-up programs to assure safe working conditions. I am calling on all personnel now to participate in the program by being careful and by reporting all falling hazards through appropriate channels. If hazards are not corrected within a reasonable time after having been reported, I hope that you will be persistent in your efforts to have them removed.

Our program, "Falls Prevention '67" will be coordinated by the Treasury Safety Council and by appropriate bureau representatives in Washington, D.C., and the field.

I urge your full support in your own selfish interest,

as well as in the interest of effective safety management in Treasury.

Henry H. Fowler

The Program instructions by which the old BS is perpetuated are delivered in many forms. Often one finds the more lengthy material giving way to short, punchy sentences accompanied by a sketch or picture. One federal agency used this method quite effectively in preparing an early Program for telling secretaries how to do things. The detailed procedures, bound under one cover, went into such things as a large-letter reminder to "KEEP FILING CURRENT." To emphasize the need, figures, graphically showing the consequence of not doing so, were used:

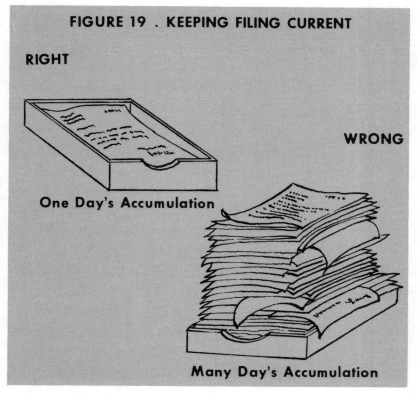

FIGURE 19 . KEEPING FILING CURRENT

RIGHT

WRONG

One Day's Accumulation

Many Day's Accumulation

This treatment of Program Instructions should be rounded out with the reminder that programmers can become too fundamental. Good information gives way to "Jane see the file. See the full file" etc. When this happens, the instructees will quickly lose interest and the information that should have been conveyed will be ignored. *Sotto Voce* references to "an idiot treatment" may be the signal that the instructions have become a little too basic.

5
THE PROGRAM CYCLE

BUREAUCRACY BEGINS writing its Programs when something needs doing to advance the commonweal or form a position. Immediately a theory is advanced and a *Study Group* is formed. Progress thereafter is made in specific steps.

Step 1. The group strives for as long as it takes to gather evidence that there is actually a need, then prepares a lengthy position paper, or justification. This consists of (a) an estimate of how much money, space and manpower is needed, and (b) a list of the benefits that will accrue when the Program is finalized. If resources aren't available, the need may be found not to be pressing and it will be held for further study until the next fiscal year. In the meantime, an interim report is made showing how much money was saved by using the "least costly approach."

Step 2. Following Study Group approval, a planning staff begins writing the tentative initial instructions, definitions, form letters, and designs the first forms. Requests for furniture, office space, and people (FOSP) are made. The first request for inputs and data are sent to those who will be affected.

Step 3. The tentative initial instructions and proposed courses of action are reproduced and sent around in formal Coordination. (Coordination is explained in detail in chapter 16.)

Step 4. Before Coordination is complete, the inputs and data requested in Step 2 begin to come in. Case numbers and code names are assigned to prevent emotional involvements that might interfere with equal treatment. This also makes it easier to reduce raw data to machine language for storing when it is no longer needed. The inputs are analyzed to see which are exactly alike and which can be made alike by adjustment. Then they are filed by category in order to convert them to outputs.

Step 5. Coordination returns begin to come in, some of which point out the need for more data. To this are added the afterthoughts that have been upgraded from second guesses to refinements. Revised forms are printed, and the original ones are augmented by a supplemental sheet. Requests for more FOSP are sent. Once in a while, the first wave of "Letters of Favorable Communication" or "Letters of Appreciation" are dispatched to fellowcrats (a) who support the justifications, (b) whose support may be needed later on, or (c) who may be in need of a boost (having been passed over at the last promotion) or (d) all three.

Step 6. Additional adjusted responses arrive and more and more of them are left to accumulate because they do not fit into any of the established processing categories. Finally, somebody affected by the lack of results makes an inquiry which will trigger a tracer action. The misfits, thus noticed, then become *special cases* for which *supplemental instructions* are written. (These become quite bulky because they must tell what makes the cases special so that subsequent ones can be recognized and processed accordingly. More requisitions for FOSP are made to equip the new branch that will be formed to deal with these special cases.)

Step 7. The new branch will store its own special cases until the trigger-and-trace sequence makes them special-special cases for which amendments to the supplemental instructions are written. These are more bulky than any others because there is more to be explained. Often they will include a certificate or two. Again, another request for FOSP is processed.

Step 8. The special case, trigger-and-trace action continues as misfits cascade down across the Program's categories until all but a few drop, pinball-like, into the System. These, the ones that will not fit anywhere, edge the System into one of three courses of action:

1. The cases that are of little consequence are disposed of by writing a regulation prohibiting any more of them. For example, the Bolling Air Force Base Exchange had an unusually hard time keeping a very popular brand of menthol cigarettes on hand. They sold too fast, which upset the shelf-stocking Program. The solution was explained by the girl at the cash register when she advised a customer who'd asked for the brand and couldn't get it that, "We had so much trouble keeping them on the shelf, we just quit stocking them altogether."

2. Once in a while the misfits are erroneously assumed to be the forerunners of an avalanche to come. A complete Program is written *in advance* to cope with them, but it lies dormant when the cases fail to materialize. This accounts for the existence of solutions for which there are no problems.

For instance, a Federal organization was engaged in tasks that require its members to be abroad more than they are at home. One day a report revealed that, over a two-year period, three passports had been lost by the holders during foreign assignments. From this it was concluded that there would be even greater losses in the United States because the holders, not having to carry them all the time, would mislay them. A Program was prepared which called for all passports to be stored in a central repository, and picked up when needed. Although during the next year there were more losses abroad, the anticipated losses within the U.S. did not come to pass and the Programmer was given credit for the success.

It is interesting that the System, for all its thoroughness, doesn't take kindly to such advance programming even when it's called Planning. It's compared with the little man on the train who kept throwing pinches of blue powder out of the window as he rode across Kansas. A fellow passenger asked him what he was doing, and he replied, "I'm scattering elephant powder. Keeps elephants away, you know."

"But," replied the other man in surprise, "there aren't any elephants in Kansas."

"Yes," responded the little fellow. "Effective, isn't it?"

3. The third alternative is the most common. Here, the cases that won't fit actually do call Bureaucracy's attention to something that needs to be done. Immediately a theory is advanced and a Study Group is formed. Progress thereafter is made in specific steps. (Please return to page 33, Step 1, and go through the steps again if necessary.)

As shown clearly in the diagram of the Pentagon budget steps below, Programs are designed to keep everything going in cycles. And although there are budget, promotion, planning, and other cycles, the Program Cycle is the basic one.

One senses that a tremendous amount of energy must be expended to get a new Program rolling. Everybody, doers and done-for, must perform according to the instructions or else the

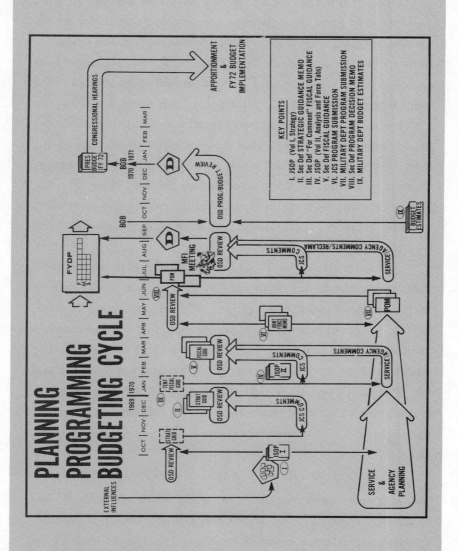

PLANNING
PROGRAMMING
BUDGETING CYCLE

KEY POINTS

I. JSOP (Vol I, Strategy)
II. Sec Def STRATEGIC GUIDANCE MEMO
III. Sec Def "For Comment" FISCAL GUIDANCE
IV. JSOP (Vol II, Analysis and Force Tabs)
V. Sec Def FISCAL GUIDANCE
VI. JCS PROGRAM SUBMISSION
VII. MILITARY DEPT PROGRAM SUBMISSION
VIII. Sec Def PROGRAM DECISION MEMO
IX. MILITARY DEPT BUDGET ESTIMATES

APPORTIONMENT
&
FY 72 BUDGET
IMPLEMENTATION

CONGRESSIONAL HEARINGS

PRES BUDGET FY 72

BOB 1970 1971

OCT | NOV | DEC | JAN | FEB | MAR | APR | MAY | JUN | JUL | AUG | SEP | OCT | NOV | DEC | JAN | FEB | MAR
1969 | 1970

OSD PROG./BUDGET REVIEW

BOB

FVDP

MFI MEETING

OSD REVIEW

POM

SERVICE

AGENCY COMMENTS/RECLAMA

JCS

OSD REVIEW

POM

SERVICE

AGENCY COMMENTS

JOINT FORCE MEMO

OSD REVIEW

FISCAL GUID

OSD REVIEW

JCS

JSOP II

COMMENTS

STRAT GUID

OSD REVIEW

JCS

COMMENTS

TENT FISCAL GUID

STRAT GUID

OSD REVIEW

JSOP I

SERVICE
&
AGENCY
PLANNING

EXTERNAL INFLUENCES

BUDGET ESTIMATES

drag could halt it. So during the early stages, all measures are taken to insure conformity.

I recall the case of an agency that had a problem with over-initiative after introducing an incentive Program by which the System paid a cash award to men making unusual contributions to their department's field. One employee paid all his own transportation, working, and living expenses to go abroad to do special research. Upon his return, his boss nominated him for the cherished award. But, it was turned down with the reminder that "It is commendable that an employee should spend his time this way, but as the work was not done at government expense, it cannot be considered for an award." Here, the Program detected, then stopped, a trend by ending the possibility of more wealthy, overly ambitious Bureaucrats "buying" their own cash awards.

Assuming that the Program eventually gets into a good spin, care must be taken to see that it does not coast. Fellowcrats, in the relaxed atmosphere of a self-sustaining System, have a tendency to write localized amendments. Instructions proliferate, fertilized by independence and initiative. The wheels and gears of Bureaucracy will be jammed by them and the System grinds to a halt. Output stops. Investigations increase, new offices are established, and the lights burn far into the night as the System's total energy goes into straightening out conflicts.

When Programs thus resolve themselves into a cataclysm, it soon becomes apparent that something needs to be done. Immediately a theory is advanced and a Study Group is formed. Progress thereafter is made in specific steps. (Please return now to page 33, Step 1, and repeat the cycle, if necessary.)

Many of my fellowcrats and I are inclined to think that the Home Mortgage Financing System may have undergone just

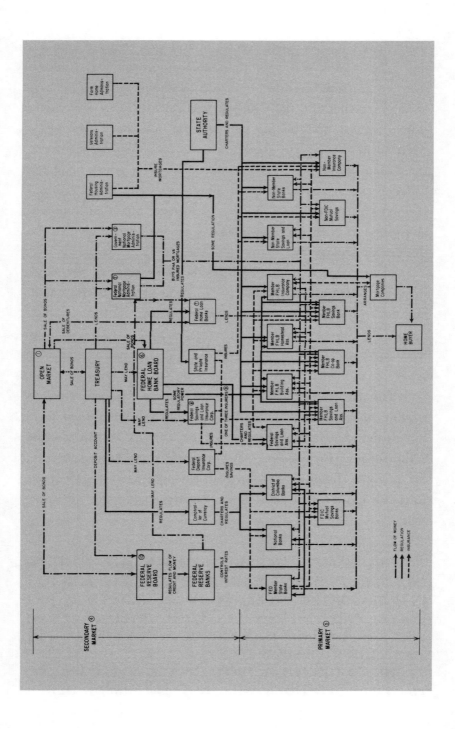

39

such a crisis a while back. Recall, if you will, that not long ago mortgage money was very tight; loan approvals just couldn't seem to get out to those who needed them. Although it was announced that the tight money was caused by an increase in prime interest rates to 8.5 percent, this may have been just a cover to hide a System breakdown. My investigations led me to the Senate Republican Party Policy Committee which had been called in as a Study Group to investigate. The group labored from August until the following February, but even then was able only to reduce the complexity to the level shown in the Committee's diagram.

In recent discussions with the Staff Director of the Committee, it was broadly hinted that this was merely an intermediate step to allow the group to catch its breath.

SCHEMATIC

The Home Mortgage Financing System cycle-interlock is trouble on a grand scale. Just how grand can be grasped from the difficulties facing one who must correct even a routine administrative breakdown. An elementary numbering mistake, for example, required a major effort on the part of a Weapons Research Center as it advised the Department of the Air Force that:

"CURRENT TECHNICAL ORDER (TO) 1-1-1 IN, INDEX, LISTS TO 1 IN-45-51 DATED 13 MAR 64, AND TO 1 IN-45-51A, DATED 29 SEPT 65, AS SUPERCEDED BY TO 1 IN-45-51 AND TO 1 IN-45-51A, BOTH DATED 17 FEB 70. THIS INFORMATION IS IN ERROR. FUTURE CHANGE TO TO 0-1-1 IN WILL SHOW TO 1 IN-45-51 DATED 13 MARCH 64 AND TO 1 IN-45-51A, DATED 29 SEP 65 AS CURRENT. 17 FEB 70 EDITIONS WILL NOT SUPERSEDE OLDER

EDITIONS UNTIL FORTHCOMING CHANGE TO 17 FEB 70 EDITIONS INCORPORATE CERTAIN INFORMATION ORIGINALLY INTENDED FOR PUBLICATION IN NEW TO 1 IN-45-55 AND TO 1 IN-45-55A, WHICH WILL NOT BE PUBLISHED."

Still, for all the strivings and difficulties, the System usually perfects its Programs before the purpose for which they were created fades away. And they stand there, gleaming monuments to equal treatment and conformity, to be cherished and clung to and kept. Indeed, one never knows when something that has served so many so well for so long may come in handy later on.

For instance, before the turn of the century when Congressmen traveled to and from Washington by stagecoach, their luggage was often lost or badly damaged. To compensate the owner, a Program was created to issue automatically to each member at each new Congress, one comb, one hairbrush, and a new trunk. That this Program is still intact is as much a tribute to the farsightedness that so accurately anticipated the airline baggage-handling problem, as to the quality of the Program itself.

6
THE PROTECTIVE VOCABULARY

"GIVE ME A CHOP off that before it goes green, will you?"[1] asked the ladycrat who works in one of the offices of the Joint Chiefs of Staff... *"We'd better totalize the whole effort before making any reclama,"*[2] suggests a memo to the officer chairing the budget meeting... *"Request you immediately effect the orderly disposition of these documents,"*[3] concludes a letter of instruction... *"The SOP requires a current 398 before OSI can do a BI on you,"*[4] advises a security clerk... *"Although standard econometric techniques are not satisfactory for estimating a regional econometric policy model, an operationally heuristic method can be used for making casual inferences on the impacts,"*[5] explains a cost study.

1. "Let us coordinate on that paper before you send it to the Joint Chiefs."
2. "Get the total price before you present your arguments."
3. "Make sure you send these to the right people."
4. "We have to have a personal history form on you before the Office of Special Investigation can check your background and character."
5. Alone, this statement is absolutely meaningless. It takes on definition according to the context of the paper or talk into which it has been inserted.

These examples of unrehearsed communications, while brief, demonstrate that the System uses a language equal to the size of its undertakings. They also show that no matter how much language training the newcomer has had, he arrives at the Bureau doors unskilled. He has only the outside world's words at his disposal, and they are woefully inadequate.

Indeed, each day Bureaucracy must work harder than ever to find just the right words as Bureaucracy outpaces the lexicographers, giving rise to the cliche, "what they are doing defies description." This was nowhere more evident than at the Scientific and Technical Directorate of the Defense Intelligence Agency some years ago. In a single wing of 12 offices and 65 people, there were eleven unabridged, 400,000-word, stand-type dictionaries, 30 desk-size dictionaries, 22 copies of Roget's Thesaurus, two Russian-English translation handbooks, and an encyclopedia of scientific terms.

Of course, there are reasons for the quest for more attention-arresting words. First, every Program, Task and Effort in which Bureaucracy is involved is *important;* all have the widest possible repercussions. Therefore they should not be portrayed otherwise through the use of common, everyday words. It is axiomatic then: if an ordinary word will do, it may not be the right one.

Next, the System's proposal usually precedes the events by months or even years. Just making the decision is a long-term proposition. So Bureaucracy speaks for the benefit of posterity as often as it does for contemporaries. That is, it writes to make sure that those who follow will understand why something was done as it was; they must not think the originators/executors stupid, or extravagant, or unimaginative. It writes also to the System's present generation to have it understand why some of the things that were supposed to come to pass had to be reevaluated and revised because they couldn't be done for the original price.

In a word, then, Bureaucrats spend most of their days *justifying* and *explaining,* these being tricky operations under the best of circumstances. So to make sure that the written word will not be misunderstood and one day rear up as an accusing finger, a special—*a protective*—vocabulary, made up of "verbal symbols," has been devised.

It is these verbal symbols, then, that demand our attention. They become The Protective Vocabulary only when properly constructed and applied. The construction is done through (a) Presuffixing, (b) Acronymizing, (c) Neologizing, (d) Honor Guard Phrases, (e) Three-Ply Weight Factors, (f) Countersinking and (g) Length for Strength. The techniques of each will be discussed in turn.

a. *Presuffixing:* This is the easiest way to a richer, more protective vocabulary. It requires only that some old stand-bys be dressed up by using the prefix "non" or the suffix "ize," or both. For example: When Gemini 9's target satellite plunged into the sea instead of going into orbit, the National Aeronautics and Space Administration described the launch as a "non-nominal operation." In another attempt elsewhere, a mechanical problem caused the countdown to be stopped long before any damage was done to the missile. This was called a "less than successful" operation. An important distinction is made here—a "non-nominal operation" is a failure that costs a whole lot more than a "less than successful" one. "Non," then, must flag a price differential and defer to a catastrophy. A few examples will clarify this point: non-standard expense—technically, the catastrophy that results when some fairly obvious costs were forgotten in the final budget; non-operational equipment—anything from bombers to typewriters which aren't

44

working because somebody forgot to order people, parts or tools to fix them. Nuclear bombs, infinitely more expensive than ordinary ones, and with a far greater catastrophy index are called "non-conventional" weapons. Likewise, an expensive catastrophy occurs if a country we don't like learns to make or buy their own non-conventional weapons. Therefore the System speaks of "non-proliferation" or "non-conventional non-proliferation."

"Ize" is a little easier to manage. It is used to add weight to a verb, or to convert a noun to a verb, thereby giving a prod to some pretty slow moving sentences. Take the word *use,* for example. Bureaucracy never utilizes use when utilize can be utilized. It also totalizes, rarely does it total. It systematizes; it seldom arranges. Programs are prioritized.

The approach to "ize-ing" is uncomplicated. Simply select a word that's been "ized" already and use it; or pick a "unized" word and "ize" it. The penultimate of the "ize" approach was reached by an Army colonel who, upon finding a project that would get along without many managers, *deprojectmanagerized* the whole thing. Logically, then, to undo any resulting catastrophy, one could easily *non-deprojectmanagerize* it.

b. *Acronymizing:* Acronymizing is the art of making words by combining the first one or two letters of a group of words. Its function is to simplify communications by reducing oft-repeated, complex titles and phrases to a set of initials. However, the acronym must spell something pronounceable; otherwise an abbreviation results, and this is too pedestrian.

The technique is to choose a word to be spelled, then construct the title to yield it. In doing so, remember that the word should be easy to pronounce and it shouldn't spell anything dirty in any language.

Dirty words sneak up even when merely writing titles and phrases without ever intending to make acronyms out of them. Since I write a lot of government papers, I always keep this rule before me: *Be Absolutely Sure That Acronyms Reflect Decency.* Indeed, an experienced acronymist converts to an acronym almost unconsciously any time he sees two or more words that are capitalized or appear to have been assembled more for their first letters than their meaning.

A good acronym will also convey the spirit or purpose behind the structure represented in the initials. AID, for example, can mean Agency for International Development (excellent), or Americans of Indian Descent (adequate). Not quite so direct but with a more ethereal quality is VISTA, Volunteers in Service to America. EAR refers to Education Amateur Radio, and on and on.

Of all the acronyms, though, OEO, Office of Economic Opportunity, warrants special attention because of the unique way it is supposed to have been created. I was told that it was derived from the first words spoken by the President when he heard how much it was going to cost: "OOOHooooooooo-EEEEEEeeeeeeeOOOOHOoooooooooo MY GOD!" The reference to Deity was dropped and a study committee looked for words to acronymize the scream. It could more easily have been called the Civilian Reemployment Institute (CRI), and when combined with Health, Education, and Welfare, there would have been a HEW and CRI.

It is good to know that the outside world is now given to acronymizing too. The women's lib movement, for example, has an organization called WITCH—Women's International Terrorists Conspiracy from Hell. Even students are applying the principles with some skill. Undergraduates from the University of

Chicago formed a men's group called Students Project for Equal Rights for Men (SPERM) and another is named Grateful Americans Supporting Pollution (GASP).

Despite the apparent simplicity, one should not conclude that acronymizing is easy. Aside from accidentally creating men's room graffiti, other embarrassments can arise. The Geodesic Intelligence and Mapping and Research and Development Agency, GIMRADA, has received letters sent to Jim Rada, or a Dr. James Rada.

By now one may believe there is nothing left to improve in the art of building acronyms. However, those with a natural talent will soon be making acronyms from acronyms, and using a computer to do it.

c. *Neologizing:* This method is worked best when old words are given new life through changing their spelling, pronunciation, or both. Recently, the word *reclama* has entered this category. It is Bureaucracy's derivation of the word *reclame* (ra klam'). *Covert* (the means by which the Russians steal our secrets), Webster says, is pronounced as though it came from *cover*. However, since it is the opposite of *overt,* it is pronounced by the System as ko' vert. *Comptroller,* once kon trol' er, is now pronounced exactly as it is spelled. This is more logical since comptrollers generally work around money which is sometimes tabulated on comptometers. So people who are associated with comptometers should be called komp trol' ers. (This was the explanation offered when the modern pronunciation was traced.)

While coining new words is a gratifying experience, the probability of success is very small since it's an individual effort. Each day, though, as Bureaucracy's writings will bear out, thousands try. My own attempts, while in no way paths to success, will indicate routes not to be taken.

47

For example, quite early in my career I suggested that since there is one Chief of Staff for each service, and when working as a single body they are known as the Joint Chiefs of Staff, they should be called the "Chieves of Staves." My idea got no place; I was told that *staves* were associated with whiskey barrels and that this would be inappropriate for such an august body. I reclammed by asking how they got by with *Joint,* but have received no reply to this day.

In fact, the only words I've coined came about accidentally through spelling and typographical errors. These burn for one brief letter or report, then fade away, however. It happens most often when I'm confronted with the decision whether to use an "a", "e" or "i": e.g., reimburs e? a? i? ble, manag e? a? i? ble, etc. I tried very hard to get Bureaucracy to accept an entirely new letter which would incorporate all three in one symbol—

Then if one weren't sure which letter to use, the tri-letter could be struck, thus saving dictionary time. It would also stop the business of final copies of formal letters coming back rudely marked, "This word is spelled with an 'e'."

The difficulties I've had with spelling have driven me into examining the ground rules. I find them singularly antiquated and not at all responsive to modern needs. For instance, while the spelling is done according to derivation and pronunciation, it also assumes that the words will be put on paper *by hand!* No consideration is given to this, the age of the typewriter, and to the fact that the letters on the keyboard do not all line up with the natural position of the fingers. Therefore, if on 13 November 1982, everybody will work for government, everybody must either type or have their work typed for them. So why not design the words so they can be spelled more easily using the typewriter.

Under this system, *the* and *and* would become *teh* and *adn; other* would become *thoer* or *ohter,* and so on to a more practical language.

d. *Honor Guard Phrases:* Bureaucracy frequently uses certain stylized groups of words to overcome the handicaps imposed by the outside world's lack of linguistic versatility. "It is requested that . . . " and "It is the considered opinion of this . . . " are common examples.

These are entirely administrative in character and are used to lead the reader gradually into the subject with a little touch of ceremony. I like to think of these selected phrases as a sort of honor guard. They don't really add a lot to what has to be done, but they lend color and dignity. Sprinkled here and there, they can convert a one or two sentence travesty into a rather profound piece of communication.

Most honor guard expressions are long standing, having

been forged out of the outside world's words years ago. I estimate, too, that there are about 124 such honor guard phrases—too many to list here. However, if a start is offered in this text, each fellowcrat can add to it and keep his own until a standardized set is published.

I assume that eventually such a catalogue will be published for I made the suggestion quite some time ago. I proposed that each expression be given a numerical designator which drafters would use in preparing material for secretaries to type. The secretary, having a similar list, would refer to the number and type the corresponding phrase. Below are a few for starters.

Numerical Designator (ND)	Honor Guard Phrases (HGP)
1	It is requested that . . .
2.	It is further requested that . . .
3	Effect the orderly disposition of . . .
4.	. . . orderly disposition of . . .
5.	It is the purpose of . . . .
6.	Be effected . . .
7.	Take immediate action to . . .
8.	It is the considered opinion of . . .
9.	Proper measures be taken to preclude . . .
10.	For submission to proper coordinating and action elements . . .
11.	It is therefore concluded that . . .
12.	It has come to the attention of . . .
13.	. . . costly and time consuming . . .

Now, putting a few of them to use, a draft would read:

"1 your office 7 prepare 10 the customary requests for bids. 2 the 4 all subsequent correspondence 6 since 8 this office that budget restrictions will require that 9 13 errors."

Once the manual is accepted and distributed, Bureaucracy can look forward to the day when the phrases and their numbers will be computerized. The drafter can then mark a few base words on a punch card, slide it in a slot at his desk, and a printed draft will appear immediately at the stenographer's desk where she can type the initial final copy without difficulty.

e. *Three-Ply Weight Factors:* They also serve which just add weight. Indeed, certain combinations of verbal symbols are used to add profundity to lightweight communications by furnishing that corpulent, well-tailored look that spells importance. Properly used, Three-Ply Weight Factors such as "integrated management options" or "systematized digital mobility" can make a sentence impressive without one's having to read it all the way through.

Three-Ply Weight Factors are constructed by selecting a base word, then modifying it with two plys of description. Polysyllables are preferable although monosyllables are acceptable if they have heavy implications; e.g., life, death, birth, tax, etc.

The table below is furnished as a starter. The base ply words are listed on the right; the modifiers are in the first two columns. Select the base word, then add two plys of profundity by selecting at random from ply 1 and ply 2 respectively. Use of "and" is optional.

Ply 1	Ply 2	Ply 3
Integrated	Management	Options
Total	Compatible	Hardware
Systematized	Organizational	Flexibility
Parallel	Monitored	Capability
Functional	Reciprocal	Mobility
Responsive	Effective(ness)	Dollar
Operational	Logistical	Concept
Relevant	Transitional	Time-phase
Optimal	Incremental	Projection
Synchronized	Digital	Programming
Balanced	Policy	Contingency

51

Complex	Changing	Objectives
Cost	Benefit	Analysis(es)

Suppose, now, one were asked to prepare a paper on purchasing missile parts. He would add weight to "parts" by making it "hardware" (base ply), then insert the profundity by selecting from plys 1 and 2, "integrated" and "logistical" respectively. Thus "parts" becomes "integrated logistical hardware." Or one may discuss the "operational management contingency" associated with "functional and incremental hardware." Thus with a little imagination and the preceding table as a foot-hold, even the newest tyrocrat can more than uphold the importance of whatever task he's striving over.

f. *Countersinking:* Any point worth making is worth making over and over again. Bureaucracy, more than any other organization, recognizes this as another fundamental of communication. To countersink an idea, one simply gives a little off-the-cuff elaboration on a word which everybody understands pretty well anyway. It reassures the reader (or listener) that the user knows exactly what it is he's writing or speaking about.

Only a single example is needed to demonstrate. The following excerpt from one of the annual fire prevention lectures so popular in the military should do.

" . . . the ravages of fire! I don't mean the ordinary kind of fire that burns in the fireplace or in the gas jets or in the charcoal broiler on the patio—the friendly fire that heats our coffee. I mean the destructive kind that destroys buildings and burns down homes and even entire cities. That's the kind of fire I'm talking about."

Countersinking is done only on words that are clearly understood in the first place. This leaves the user free to expound without fear of introducing some misunderstanding. And although the act of explaining has been purified in the Agencies, it is seldom done without provoking some misunderstanding somewhere. Therefore, whenever one has an opportunity to explain something further without causing more misunderstanding, he may do so using the countersink method, knowing that it will be well received.

g. *Length for Strength:* To any Maestrocrat worth his files, it would come as no surprise to learn that Ernest Hemingway and John Steinbeck et al. couldn't get a job with government. They wrote in short sentences that inundated the reader with ideas and concepts, leaving him no time to get a good grip on one part of an idea before another was thrown at him.

Indeed, it is a fact that all the skills developed in building new words, adding weight, and countersinking would be wasted if Bureaucracy's complex Programs were dribbled out in quick miserly sentences. The reason is clear. Once the reader's attention is directed along a chain of thought, it's best to keep him going for as long as possible. Interruptions with periods provide cracks through which the mind will slip for a bit of wandering and loafing.

Reading is speeded up considerably, too, because as with anything else in Bureaucracy, there is an inertia associated with changes of pace while starting and stopping, and thus if ideas are presented in short sentences and short words the start-stop inertia is multiplied many times as opposed to long, strong sentences which avoid the staccato delivery allowing much more intelligence to be gleaned from a single scanning, as one may have noticed in reading this particular example.

The construction techniques just explored are only the fascicles of a great language. Their integration into the rich, easy flowing Protective Vocabulary depends upon the skill used in the application. And for convenience, certain of these—Proclamations, Universal Responses, Principle of Amorphism—will be explained in the following chapters.

7

TO BUILD A PROCLAMATION

USING THE POST CARD size diagram upon which the lady at the information desk has traced my route, I set out on another excursion into the Pentagon. I climbed ramps and stairs, matched wall colors to floor numbers, awed my way in and out of concentric rings of offices and hurried along the halls until I stood proudly before the corridor which, according to the diagram, was the last leg. Somewhere just ahead lay room 5E539, the office I wanted.

At first I was too flushed with success to notice the bold sign placed squarely in the middle of the corridor entrance. However, the chain stretched across just behind it reminded me to look.

"THIS PASSAGEWAY HAS BEEN MADE NON-CONDUCIVE TO UTILIZATION FOR AN INDEFINITE PERIOD"

the notice said.

Ordinarily, I would have stepped over the barrier and gone on anyway. I didn't see anything to stop me; certainly nothing dangerous. But I didn't. Something about the quality of the sign made me pause. It was, in fact, quite different from the quiet-tempered "Hall Temporarily Closed" that one might expect, and which would equate to the plain "No Smoking" warnings that are noted only briefly before lighting up, unless they say "Positively!" And that's exactly what this sign said to me—Positively! Actually, it sounded just a little bit angry.

As I wandered around trial and erroring by another route, I thought about the sign and decided that its deterrent impact lay in the impression made by the ultra-official, very formal language employed. And after that I observed that there were notices like it all over the place, not only in the Pentagon, but throughout Bureaucracy. Moreover, they weren't limited to placards; they appeared in the form of messages, letters, memos, bulletin board postings, and even in the phone directories. For example, the State Department's phone book for the Agency for International Development (AID) lists a number for the "Associate Assistant Administrator in the Office of Assistant Administrator for Administration."

Indeed, it was like looking up a word you'd never heard before, then suddenly hearing it used ten different times the next day.

This particular utilization of the Protective Vocabulary—proclaiming—is the oldest and most visible application. It was a case of something being so omnipresent that I never noticed it. Of course I had often used the technique because I sensed more than understood that this was the way. Still, until that day in the Pentagon when I became studiously aware of the method, all my previous work in notice writing had been done purely by rote. Realizing this, I discovered why so much of my material was rewritten before being allowed into the System.

Proper vocabulary or not, unless one has a genuine feel for preparing this most elementary type of Program material, rote is the only way, and success will be at most a matter of pure luck. Clearly, luck or not, no rote notice writer ever got his signs in the Pentagon corridors any more than a rote pianist ever played Carnegie Hall. In all cases, class tells; or in a more proclamatory tone, supereminence evinces.

The following notice concerning coffee breaks, prepared in San Luis Obispo County, California, is a classic in the field of Proclaiming.

RESOLUTION REGARDING COFFEE BREAKS

The following resolution is now offered and read:

WHEREAS, short breaks in the work schedule of employees, which are commonly known as coffee breaks, are desirable in promoting the efficient performance of work during working hours; and

WHEREAS, such coffee breaks are further desirable in the interest of employee's morale; and

WHEREAS, suitable regulation of such coffee breaks is necessary in organizations with large numbers of employees,

NOW, THEREFORE, BE IT RESOLVED AND ORDERED by the Board of Supervisors of the County of San Luis Obispo, State of California:

1. That employees of the County of San Luis Obispo be, and they hereby are permitted to take one coffee break in the morning, and one coffee break in the afternoon of each work day.

2. That such coffee breaks be, and they hereby are

limited to a period of 15 minutes duration each, for the morning and afternoon breaks.

3. That the Department Heads of the various County Departments be, and they hereby are directed to schedule such breaks, and to regulate the frequency and duration of the same pursuant to the above.

4. That the Clerk of this Board be, and he hereby is directed to transmit copies of this resolution to each Department Head.

Likewise, I cannot help but feel that Marie Antoinette and many of her friends might have kept their heads had she said "Let them eat cake" with the same formal expansiveness as did the Western Electric Company in the proclamation memo they prepared:

WESTERN ELECTRIC

North Andover, Mass.

November 11, 1969

TO ALL DEPARTMENT CHIEFS

On November 18, 1969 the Company will observe its 100th anniversary. In honor of this occasion the first rest period for each shift will be extended to twenty minutes.

Prior to the first rest period each department will send one person, for each twenty-five employees in the department, to a pre-assigned cafeteria to pick up cake which will be distributed at rest period.

The plant will be divided in half, starting at the main lobby entrance and running straight down the rear of the plant. Departments on the Lawrence side of this dividing line will pick up cake in the south cafeteria; those on the Haverhill side will pick up at the north cafeteria.

During the period from November 12, 1969, through November 17, 1969, departments will pick up tickets at the Public Relations Office for their employees. There will be two types of tickets; pink tickets for 25 pieces of cake and a yellow ticket for odd numbers.

Example: If a department has 80 employees (including supervisors) they will pick up three pink and one yellow ticket. The yellow will be marked five employees and signed by individual department chief.

Schedule and procedures to be followed on November 18, 1969, is:

SHIFT HOURS	CAKE PICK-UP TIME	REST PERIOD
7:00 to 3:30	8:00 — 9:00	9:20 — 9:40
8:00 to 4:45	9:00 — 10:00	10:00 — 10:20
Second Shift	4:45 — 5:20	5:20 — 5:40

Third Shift — All employees go to the south cafeteria from 1:30 — 1:50 A.M., where cake will be served.

In addition to the above, a commemorative book mark will be given to each employee on November 18, 1969. These will be distributed through your Assistant Manager's Office.

8

THE UNIVERSAL
RESPONSE (UR)

THIS TREATMENT OF the Protective Vocabulary must include another of its fundamental applications, the Universal Response.

I recall once attending a conference on Industrial Funding (IF). It was a big formal affair held in Washington on a sunny mid-August afternoon. We had just finished a two-martini luncheon and had returned to the quiet of the plush conference room, to learn that the air conditioner had failed in our absence. The heat, the pressure of the previous days, and the overtime that went with them pressed hard upon me. To help me concentrate on what the speaker was saying, I closed my eyes to shut out the distractions. The speaker made his presentation with an unhurried, even-toned, steady delivery which I found most soothing. Dwelling at length on a point he'd made earlier, and deep in thought, I lost the thread of his talk. Suddenly I was jolted loose, as it were, by hearing my name called for confirmation of a salient conclusion. Since I was the chairman, I sensed that the fellowcrat would be embarrassed were I to ask him to go over the matter again. To spare him, I resorted to a Universal Response (UR), e.g., "That's certainly worth considering. I think, too, that a standard balance concept is not always satisfactory for unique operational time-phasing, especially where incremental effectiveness is universally determined by unmonitorable excursions beyond the three-sigma limits." Convinced of my support he concluded his presentation with revived confidence.

I maintain a repertoire of URs for use at meetings, conferences, or informal gatherings. I've selected one with which the tyrocrat may begin. It may be used freely in speaking or writing.

"A unified professional public affairs structure would provide the long sought articulating factor in the concatenation of its agencies, and afford its constituencies the effective efficient anticipation and satisfaction of their information needs."

The tyrocrat should have no misgivings at all about the effectiveness of such URs since they are important to conducting business without rancor. Indeed, the Good Ole Boy in us demands that we not deliberately hurt anybody's feelings. Always, it is better to leave a fellowcrat cold, than to leave him hot under the collar.

9

THE PRINCIPAL OF AMORPHISM

THERE IS AN ULTIMATE state of Bureaucracy wherein those who are served by the System will be caused more trouble by not complying with the Program than if they did, whether they need the service or not. I have elected to call this state *Buarchy* because it is the inevitable predecessor to anarchy. Traceable through the way the System gives its orders, the evolution is explained in this chapter.

Telling people—fellowcrats or people from the outside world—to do or not to do something is one of Bureaucracy's main jobs. This act of directing constitutes an infringement on the directee's time because it calls for a change in established routines. And although issuing orders is commonplace, Bureaucracy still does it using three methods instead of just one.

(a) Pleading. Many tyrocrats, and maestrocrats who have mellowed under the warmth of coming retirement, tend to be solicitous in their writing. Words like "cordially" and "please" creep in, and deferential routes to getting things done are taken. The System frowns on such an approach because it works only with those who would do what was requested anyway. Others simply ignore the request and wait for something stronger to come along to show that the System means it.

(b) Command. Throughout all ages and levels of Bureaucrats, there are those who mistake their respective position for one of authority. Their Program instructions reek of the "By God, I'm king and you will . . . " totalitarianism. Of course, this doesn't work either because in contemporary Bureaucracy, the people who have the kingly positions are too far removed from the problems to provide the lever or command.

(c) Principle of Amorphism. The presence of beggars and kings within the System causes the Principle of Equal Treatment to be violated. What, indeed, could be more antipodal than one person receiving a direct order while his neighbor is tendered a plea? Fortunately the Principle of Amorphism, properly applied, eliminates this dilemma.

It is done first by envisioning the recipients as a crowd of shapes drifting across the length and breadth of the outside world, across the layers and echelons of the Agencies. Once no personalities or faces are identifiable, the right blend of impersonalism can be achieved without fear of hurting anybody's feelings. Nobody will take umbrage because nobody has occasion to feel singled out. In turn the shapes "out there" will look back across an expanse of Bureaucracy and see that the source is equally amorphous. It will do them no good to get angry because there is no one individual to blame—just the System. Compliance follows for one has long since learned that fighting the System can be a long, involved struggle ending, at best, in a pyrrhic victory.

The Principle of Amorphism is at its best when used to accommodate those few who tend to ignore some long-standing, everyday directive. That is, when two or three people do something wrong, write a directive giving everybody hell. Such usage avoids mentioning names, and may also stop somebody who is on the verge of a violation.

Getting the renegades back on course is only one use of the Principle of Amorphism. It is also perfectly suited to setting the course in the first place. Although merely another form of Proclamation writing, this application has a key adjunct. Usually, the amorphism used causes some directees to assume the rule applies to "the other fellow." Or it may make them feel that nobody would notice if an order were ignored. Perhaps, too, they may believe that it will be all right to comply until things blow over, then restore the status quo. Therefore it is necessary to make the directees feel that something will be done to them unless they comply. Or more candidly, there's got to be a threat.

It is through this, the manner in which the threat is put across, that one can trace the organizations' evolution in Buarchy.

Unlike the "Firing In Progress. Do Not Enter" sign on the rifle range, or the downtown "ONE WAY" street sign, most situations do not have an intrinsic warning; it must be supplied. The manner by which this is accomplished maps the evolution.

A subscription renewal notice from a national news magazine asks, *"Please, do not fold or tear this card."* This is almost entirely non-Bureaucratic. Called level one, it is peculiar to business in competition for profit.

However, a bill from the Arlington County, Virginia, Water

Department bore the instruction, *"IMPORTANT. Do Not Fold, Staple, or Mutilate This Stub."* Here the expression "cut your water off" changes from a figurative to a literal sense, and will probably induce compliance when the "late payment" charges will not. This is level two; it is common to public utilities, which, to exist, must toe a semi-Bureaucratic line.

The Virginia Division of Motor Vehicles illustrates the third level. Their license tags renewal application bears the Proclamation, *"DO NOT MUTILATE, DETACH OR USE PINS OR STAPLES IN THESE CARDS."* Bicycles, long walks, jogging and public transit loom ominously behind the "DO NOT." This, of course, is pure Bureaucracy. Straightforward, addressed to everybody, and no nonsense. And no outright threat.

We arrive now at level four—Buarchy.

As with other instructions in this text, an example will help the reader to comprehend. I have used "KEEP OUT" on all levels so that proper application of the Principle of Amorphism will shine through.

Level one: (profit makers) "Please Do Not Enter."

Level two: (semi-Bureaucratic) "No Admittance."

Level three: (Bureaucratic, amorphous) "CAUTION. CONTROLLED AREA. It Is Unlawful to Enter This Area Without Special Permission." or "YOU ARE HEREWITH ADVISED THAT SPECIAL PERMISSION IS MANDATORY FOR PROCEEDING BEYOND THIS POINT."

Level four: (Buarchy) *"TRESPASSERS WILL BE SHOT!!"* (Note: If the shots are returned, Buarchy will have evolved into anarchy.)

As a check on how well one has mastered this technique, I suggest he attempt to amorphize the 1936 mobilization notice posted by Haile Selassie when his country was invaded by Italy:

"EVERYONE WILL NOW BE MOBILIZED AND ALL BOYS OLD ENOUGH TO CARRY A SPEAR WILL BE SENT TO ADDIS ABABA. MARRIED MEN WILL TAKE THEIR WIVES TO CARRY FOOD AND COOK. THOSE WITHOUT WIVES WILL TAKE ANY WOMEN WITHOUT A HUSBAND. WOMEN WITH SMALL BABIES NEED NOT GO. THE BLIND, THOSE WHO CANNOT WALK, OR FOR ANY REASON CANNOT CARRY A SPEAR ARE EXEMPT. ANYONE FOUND AT HOME AFTER THE RECEIPT OF THIS ORDER WILL BE HANGED."

10

THE PROTECTIVE VOCABULARY: GENERALIZED PROPER AND NON-PROPER UTILIZATION

JUDGES 15:16 TELLS HOW Sampson slew a thousand men with the jawbone of an ass. Regretfully, this same feat is being duplicated regularly as the jawbones of contemporary asses swing into action. For example: I had been assigned to a new office, in a supervisor's slot. After I'd adjusted myself in the swivel chair behind a beat-up desk, I began listening to the briefings prepared by the technicians, thereby hoping to get a broad idea of the problems I'd be facing. Suddenly, one of my new charges approached one of the men standing beside the desk. Without acknowledging my existence other than a quick downward glance out of the corner of his eye, he said to the man: "Sir. An ECM ALT-6 went NRTS. The SJR and WO 48 called for a priority one, but the 829-2 is missing. Could I get an OCX from PI till we 446 a new one?"

This was the protective vocabulary at its best. But it was being prostituted! The sole purpose was to remind me about how much more others knew about the place than I did. However I recognized the ploy for what it was, and put a stop to any further such magniloquence by asking the man to repeat the request to me, but to do so slowly so I could write it down and have it interpreted when I wasn't busy.

I could have easily chimed in, countering with the PV utilized at my prior duty station in England; even could've dropped a few British verbal symbols just to embarrass him. However, there is nothing so distressing as two grown Bureaucrats squared off and hurling acronymns, abbreviations, numbers and neologisms indiscriminately at each other, neither knowing what the other is talking about. Such confrontations are degrading and should be avoided.

Three methods are employed when the PV is ill-utilized to impress somebody. Least common is the direct approach where the impressee is addressed face to face. Most common is the one-sided pitch where the impressor addresses a third party, and the impressee is the audience. Last is the bilateral pitch where the impressor employs a shill who responds in kind, leaving the impressee to catch it from both sides.

If the impressee wishes to disengage, he may ask for the discourse to be submitted in writing. Or, just as soon as the opportunity arises, say a word or two about " . . . haven't been here too long yet, and it's going to take me a little time to get my bearings. There'll be a lot of questions, I guess." Or if one feels one must, then: "Yeah. I had something similar to that at my last job on the West Coast. We had this by-pass 423 . . . " etc.

Here, one may ask, "Should the Protective Vocabulary ever be used as a catalyst for confusion?" The answer, of course, is yes.

Throughout the System there are those who sometimes deliberately, sometimes inadvertently, practice Program homicide under the guise of euthanasia. They amass huge clusters of obvious reasons why a Program is no longer worth keeping alive, and present them in outside-world terms. Because these are foreign they are mistakenly thought to be couriers of purely logical courses of action.

When one's Program is under such an attack he is within his rights to appeal his case. He may bundle together all the many small arguments to the contrary, wrap them in the most massive verbal symbols available and present them to the approving authorities. He can hope that the sheer force of words will outweigh the obvious reasons to kill his PET Project.

Circumstances often favor such a tactic. The approving authorities are always too busy to become familiar with anything but the broadest aspects of any Program. Still, they will not wish to appear ignorant, so to be safe, they most likely will resolve any doubts by keeping the Program intact. Usually, there will be a few minor changes made just to show the Program advocate that he can't have it all his own way.

Reprieves of this sort are nearly always certain provided the Program's advocates can use the Protective Vocabulary properly. The approving authorities must understand that they are being supplied with all the details which, because of their high position and busy schedule, are too nuts-and-bolts for them to fool with. Put another way: to be on the safe side, authorities will approve anything they do not understand. And they do so with confidence since there are comfortable precedents in their predecessors' decisions.

Many things are monuments to the protection inherent in the glorious Protective Vocabulary: airplanes that have wing trouble, rifles that jam, bridges over dry rivers are but a few. They serve also to remind the Outside World that it is the building of the airplane, the rifles, and the bridges that's the important thing. Get the tangible evidence of the Program's existence before the eyes of the public and keep it alive. After the monuments are standing tall and proud, the purposes they are to serve can be whipped into line.

11
EXPLAINING THINGS

WE NOW TURN TO the workaday strivings of Bureaucracy—explaining things in Support of Programs (SOP).

One day I sat waiting in a fellowcrat's office while he struggled through his mid-mid-morning coffee break. Looking idly around the small, well-packed office, I studied the paraphernalia he'd gathered around him for atmosphere. My eyes quickly fell on a neatly lettered sign under the glass on his desk: "I know you believe you understand what you think I said, but I am not sure you realize that what you think you heard is not what I meant."

I knew right away that he meant it to be a little touch of humor, and I smiled as I should have. But as sometimes happens in Bureaucracy, humor is no more than a sly way of holding aloft some shortcoming or irritation. It was then that I realized that only about 6.265% of the System's writing went into PET Project protection and disguising orders; the other 93.735% was devoted to explaining:

a. How to do things.

b. How things were done before.

c. Why things that were done can be done over better.

d. Why things that are going to be done need not be done.

e. Why things that are not going to be done need to be done.

f. Why what is on hand should be kept, and how it can be justified.

g. Why things need to be updated or modernized, and how it can be justified.

h. How in any of the conditions above, more money, space and people might be needed.

Although it is very rare that all of these topics will be found in the same set of explanations, they are not uncommon in multiples of three or four.

Classically, good explanations follow ironclad axioms. First, simple things are to be explained in simple, understandable words; complex things are to be explained in complex, understandable words. This may sound paradoxical, but the need for conformity, consistency, and equal treatment applies here too. Also, explanations should start at the beginning, not in the middle of a subject. Only the most skilled Maestrocrat can successfully indulge in retroflex explanations as the following example, taken from the Connecticut Driver's Manual, shows:

"LICENSE RENEWAL: Your first license expires on the last day of the month in which your next birthday occurs unless your next birthday will occur in the same month you are tested or in either of the two succeeding months in which case your first license expires one year from the last day of the month in which your birthday occurs. A first license will not be issued for less than 4 nor more than 15 months. You will then be issued a renewal for one or two years depending on whether you were born in an odd-numbered year or in an even-numbered year; thereafter, you will renew your license every two years—in an odd-numbered year if you were born in an odd-numbered year, or in an even-numbered year if you were born in an even-numbered year."

And finally, there should be no threat implied.

* * *

When the growing Bureaus learned how important it was that things be explained properly and thoroughly, they set about explaining the things that were already in the field, but which needed clearing up. But since those doing the clearing up lacked both experience and precedents, a lot of their work had to be explained in more detail too. This led to a number of entirely new Programs, Projects and Tasks which produced other Programs, Projects and Tasks as the things that were explained in the preceding Programs were re-explained in subsequent Programs. In an operation that size, there were bound to be excesses, and soon Bureaucracy began to accumulate paper with no purpose. This wasted storage space and in fact, reduced the value of the filing cabinets.

Fortunately, Bureaucracy saw what was happening and started over again, this time at the beginning. In doing so it asked that Bureaucrats reduce the volume of files by writing only what is *necessary*. The way was shown, I believe, by the Defense Intelligence Agency. In their correspondence manual under the paragraph entitled "Responsibilities" they launched the explain-it-all-the-first-time method of explaining. Starting at rock bottom they reminded: "Any act of communication involves three necessary components: (a) a 'communicator' who has meaning to transmit; (b) a 'symbol' or a 'system of symbols' that carries the meaning; and (c) a 'receptor' who receives the symbol and translates it into meaning in his own mind. In writing, no communication occurs unless your reader is able to understand your thoughts—gets your message. The message must have meaning to the reader . . . " Then it declared, "Decide whether a written communication is necessary."

The new bedrock approach caught on and one after another Federal, State and Local Bureaucracies tried their hand with startling results. For example: Title 5 of the California Administrative Code (concerning Education) explains: "TENSES, GENDER AND NUMBER. As used in this subchapter, the present tense includes the past and future tenses, and the future, the present; the masculine gender includes the feminine, and the feminine, the masculine; and the singular number the plural and the plural, the singular."

The Wyoming Highway Department explained "In order to avoid cumbersome and confusing repetition of expressions in these specifications, it is provided that whenever anything is or is to be done, if as, or when, or where 'contemplated, required, determined, directed, specified, authorized, ordered, given, designated, indicated, considered necessary, deemed necessary, permitted, reserved, suspended, established, approval, approved, disapproved, acceptable, unacceptable, suitable, accepted, satisfactory, unsatisfactory, sufficient, insufficient, rejected, or condemned,' it shall be understood as if the expression were followed by the words 'by the engineer' or 'to the engineer.' "

At an Army Post in the east, a memo was circulated that set out some ground rules for local Programs. It specified that "The Commandant objects to the use of the term 'verbal orders' when 'oral orders' is intended. He points out that verbal orders can be either written or oral since both employ verbs."

The trend extended into the historically staid Army Regulations (AR). AR 37-102 explains "ad. Subproject. A subproject is a project divided into subprojects. Subprojects are for use in connection with budget programming and execution. For accounting and reporting purposes, subprojects will be considered as projects."

An explanation on a Department of Health, Education, and Welfare card that asked if the recipient wanted to be kept on the mailing list, told how it could be done: "If not returned within 30 days, we will assume you are no longer interested in this service and you will be removed from our lists. If you do not wish to receive any U.S. Office of Education publications, please check this box."

Once in a while in the realm of explanations the Bureaus produce a work that exposes new horizons, reaching out to grasp the reader and to lead him gaily along virgin territory in lucidity. Such is the HEW book entitled *Environmental Health Practices in Recreational Areas,* a classic in simple explanations of simple subjects. Written for Bureaucracy as well as for the outside world, it courageously tells of the little but important things to consider when planning an outing or selecting campsites. Page 135 emphasizes that the camper should be as far as possible from "railroads, airports, truck routes, factories, and other sources of noise which detract from a restful and peaceful environment." The book recommends that campsites have pure water and drinking fountains, and that "the height of the fountain at the drink level should be such as to be most convenient to persons utilizing the fountain." Not wishing to leave anything unexplained, there are reminders that "Insects crawling into the ears of outdoorsmen sometimes create painful conditions that require surgical procedures for removal." Comfort stations are to be built "with separate compartments for men and women." There's a warning that "mosquito bites may cause such discomfort to visitors in some recreational areas that the areas are unused or full enjoyment is not possible." And on page 84, below a photo of a swimming pool, there is a caption saying starkly "Outdoor Swimming Pool."

Having now somewhat established the idea, let us turn briefly to the principal vehicles by which the explanations are disseminated. I refer to the formal means—*studies* and *reports*. And since data for these often arrive carefully tabulated on *forms*, some discussion of these will be included also.

12
STUDIES

OF ALL THE PROGRAM vehicles by which Bureaucracy explains things and thereby keeps the System going, *Studies* seem to have the worst reputation by far. And even though they are not the most common products, they are the most pre-eminent.

Evidence that their ultimate fall from grace was precipitated as recently as the mid-19th century is found in one Leslie Stephen's 1865 *Sketches From Cambridge.* In it he claimed, "But if you wish at once to do nothing and be respectable nowadays, the best pretext is to be at work on some profound study." This sneering indictment was made, most likely, after circa-1850 Bureaucrats became careless and made a mockery out of preparing the Studies of the times. To put it simply, they failed to give enough thought, time or care to achieving just that precise balance among bulk, binding, proper titling, and statement of purpose that spells *importance,* and identifies the Study as a Product of Thought (POT).

Shortly after Stephen's attack, some conscientiousness returned to Study making. They are now at a point where they have nearly resumed their rightful place, even though there is some occasional backsliding; contemporaries, for example, have seized on the expedient of taking simple *reports* (see chapter 13), padding them well, then passing them off as Studies.

The true Study has a number of identifying features. First of all, it *looks* solid. It has a certain character that seems to say that from six months to two years of top talent went into it.

While bulk is often mistakenly looked upon as the *prime* ingredient, it is not of such importance. In fact, I judge from the Studies with which I work (and help produce) that it is common for them to run from 350 to 500 pages. Each page is typewritten, double-spaced, one side of the paper only, and has a wide margin all around.

Studies also come in volumes. It is not unusual to see the number of volumes go as high as seven or eight, and it is rare that there are ever less than two. Moreover, each volume boasts its own:

a. Table of Contents
b. Summary of what was in the preceding volumes
c. Glossary of Terms
d. A number of individual chapters or sections, each with a summary and a small list of definitions
e. List of Acknowledgements
f. Bibliography
g. Exhibits
h. Appendix
i. Annex
j. Index

The cover is another important feature. Each volume usually, but not always, has a cover that is a lot thicker and of a somewhat better quality than the paper on the inside. This is more true if the government has made up the bindings. If produced by a civilian "think tank" or other contractor study group, the cover will be printed on very high quality, relatively thick paper, and laminated or sheathed in transparent plastic which gives a lustrous, almost exotic, cast. In the matter of bindings, irrespective of the type cover, the minimum to be expected is a semi-permanent arrangement.

To be distinguished, more than just physical glamour is needed. For this reason, extreme care is given to selecting a *title* and to *stating the purpose*. Both must be built up to get the importance across, once the cover and the first couple of pages catch the eye. Done properly it will quell any indignation that may stem from the expensive look the Study may have about it. This happy condition comes most quickly when the purpose and title are one; it is then that the full range of consistency is achieved.

For example, I doubt seriously that any Agency would hold still for a Study on *training aids;* a report perhaps, but no more. But a section in HEW was quite happy with a $159,000 Study entitled "A Survey of Audiovisual Materials in Public Schools and Factors Influencing Their Use." Nine thousand dollars went toward a Study "to evaluate attitudes of teachers toward teaching." The Department of Agriculture made $74,000 available to "study consumer preference, usages and buying practices for potatoes," then invested $15,000 more for a "Study on Frozen French Fried Potatoes to Measure Effect of Size of Pieces on Consumer Preference." HEW again allocated $9,000 "to evaluate the hypothesis that the weight of individual subjects can be approximated with sufficient accuracy from the subject's own estimate or one given by a second source within the same household."

So it is, then, that physical attributes are just superficial elements of a good Study. When they are paramount, the end product, as will be explained now, is a Report.

13
REPORTS

CAESAR, UPON BEING ASKED by the Roman Senate how things were going in Gaul, replied, "Veni, Vidi, Vici." This was history's shortest Report: too short, no doubt, because not long after that the Senate stabbed him.

Consider the Declaration of Independence. Here was a 297-word Report on how people felt about taxes and tea breaks. Not long after it was signed, a bloody great war took place.

The fate of President Lincoln should be looked at in the context of short reports, too. His untimely death came after he delivered a 266-word State of the Union report at Gettysburg.

In contrast to these tragedies, there is the good fortune of being alive, well, and working in the Department of Agriculture, as is the case with the Maestrocrat who submitted a 27,000 word Report explaining a reduction in the price of cabbage.

Clearly, short reports are the engines of chaos. So if bulk is not paramount in Studies, it certainly is in Reports.

Good Reports can be anywhere from 75 to 300 typewritten, double-spaced pages. *Fair* Reports can be as few as 20 pages; less than 20 pages is no Report at all.

It would seem at first that a Report should be allowed to go all the way to Study size without any charges of chicanery being made. But this cannot be done. Studies are foundation stones and much is built on them. Reports, on the other hand, either go into a Study or come out of one, since most often they—

a. Explain a condition or conditions that need the System's attention.

b. Explain what can be done under the circumstances.

c. Explain why all the steps in "b" weren't applicable by the time they could be applied.

So, if Reports were passed off as Studies, the foundation would weaken and the superstructure—the System—would collapse.

Reports lack prestige in another respect. They are often the product of only one or two people, and more pedestrian still, no top talent is employed. In other words, Studies are signed by Ph.D's or Master's Degrees at a minimum; a Report can be signed by nearly anybody. And this brings up another important aspect: Reports must not look too expensive.

I recall how the United Planning Organization, Washington, D.C.'s local poverty program, began publishing a monthly report using glossy paper. However, critics wisely pointed out that "it looked much too expensive." The second issue was mimeographed on rough paper which was more in keeping with poverty planning. The "cheap" look was maintained even after it proved to be more costly since four pages printed on glossy paper were replaced by ten of the mimeographed ones.

As Bureaucracy goes, there is a tendency to do more Reports than Studies because it's cheaper. The finished products can then be stacked to show a high level of striving within the organization.

It pays to be on the safe side by sticking to Report formats admired by superiors. Individuality can lead to endless minor changes until the proper presentation is achieved. I suggest, then, that the tyrocrat check through the files for a Report that received an "A" grade, and use it as a base or guide. (The "A" will be signified if there is a penciled or inked note in the margin on the first page of text, saying "good job" or something to that effect.) In fact, if one cares to search long enough, the files will yield a Report prepared on the same subject some years back. In this case, all one must do is update a few graphs and figures, write in a few of the boss' favorite expressions, and introduce the latest of the Protective Vocabulary's verbal symbols.

Such a report will pay double dividends in that it will serve as a prototype for the fellowcrat who will follow in time to come, and who, like you, will need help.

14

FORMSMANSHIP

THE MOST SERIOUS mistake the tyrocrat can make is to assume that Forms are just a bunch of blanks waiting to be filled in, or to categorize them as the ragged-sleeved cousins to Studies and Reports. Cousins they may be. But ragged? Never!

The House Committee on Post Office and Civil Service disclosed that there are now over 360,000 different forms used by Federal Bureaucracy alone. When the total complement has been dispatched on their data collecting mission, they go forth 15 billion strong! Moreover, no fewer than 900 formsmen devote full time to looking after them.

With so many forms no wonder the recipients—the form-ees—are indifferent when filling them out. Carelessness and flippancy attest to this. Indeed, how often I've processed entries where the formee was 150 feet tall, or weighed 72 inches, or who had mothers named Edgar, or a father named Gertrude. They've had bald eyes and blue hair, and their last salary was exactly the same as their social security number.

Mind. I have nothing but contempt for the perverted humorists who use the blanks as straight lines; that is, by invariably answering "Sex" with "yes," "occasionally," "Social affairs only," etc.

Formsmanship may be defined as the use of blank spaces and questions to get the formees to pay serious attention to filling out the answers. It is a new approach, almost a science, and replaces the old methods—threats, pleas, orders to go back and do it over, rewards, packaging, and so on, all of which failed in their purpose. And today, all forms are constructed according to the five tenets of formsmanship:

a. There must be at least one question which the formee cannot answer without hunting through a lot of old records. This is accomplished by means of numbers. Everybody over 18 has at least 25 numbers assigned to him and his permits to do things. Employee numbers from the first job, 1962 license tags, World War II serial number, voting precinct, date of last X-ray are but a few. Once he invests real time, the formee will be more respectful.

b. There must be two or three blanks too small in which to permit one to write the information requested. Making the block too small forces the formee to think carefully about what he is going to say, and requires him to write unusually small.

c. One or two blanks must provide much more space than is needed. (Turning to DoD form 398, note the expanse of white labeled "Signature of Person Completing Form.")

"Signature of Person Completing Form")

This is a real thought-provoker. After one makes the entry, the leftover space causes him to spend the rest of the form wondering what he's left out. This effect can be heightened if the too-large block follows closely behind the too-small one.

d. At least one instruction should have a hint of ambiguity. For example: under "Answer All Questions In This Section," insert a black-bordered space titled "DO NOT WRITE IN THIS SPACE." The formee will invariably re-read the instructions which insures more considered answers.

e. The questions must continue until the page is filled up. Bureaucracy is as ill-disposed toward blank space on paper as it is to silence at a conference, since both are expressions of waste. Sometimes the sheet can be completed with one or two subjective questions, i.e.: "Have you ever been arrested?" for example, is a favorite of the personnel people. If in a rush, a "Remarks" section is always good, too.

Singly or in combination, these devices are certain to produce some really conscientious blank filling. This is obviously the result of careful planning, and one can see the flaw in thinking that formsmen don't know what they are doing, or if they do, just don't give a damn.

15

THE PAPER CRITERION

". . . AND WHEREAS, BEFORE, our forefathers had no other books but the score and tally, thou hast caused printing to be used; and, contrary to the king, his crown, and dignity, thou hast built a paper mill."

Thus, the problems posed by piles of paper are not new; even Shakespeare agonized over them. The House Committee on Post Office and Civil Service, while no Shakespearian company, did some contemporary agonizing in its report on modern Bureaucracy's white tide. Entitled *The Paperwork Jungle*, it disclosed that 25,000,000 cubic feet of records and Reports were hoarded away in Washington *alone!* Moreover the paper is still coming in at a rate of 1300 boxcar loads every year. That's three and a half boxcar loads every day!

I talked with some of the Committee's staffers about the impact of this. After some "fill the Pentagon and Empire State Building" comparisons, a researcher told me with emphatic indignation, "You have no idea how much that is. If a guy worked day and night throwing one sheet of paper in the Potomac every second, it'd take him 23,000 years to get rid of what's on hand now!"

That was several years ago. Since then over 2600 computers have been added to Bureaucracy. Considering their high-speed printout capability, I compute an additional 54,000 cubic feet added every day. Using this quantity and adding in the effect of all the copying machines, I estimate that the last federally owned building in the United States will be filled to capacity with files at 9:33 A.M. on 27 July 1986. All our people will be in the streets and paper will literally become Bureaucracy's master.

The rate at which government acquires additional space makes me think that others are getting a little panicky, too. The General Services Administration (GSA) reports reveal, for example, that in 1969 12.5 million square feet of space was added. Assuming eight foot ceilings, this makes 100 million cubic feet of offices available for storing files. Still, this could be only a temporary solution; zoning laws and availability of real estate would choke off the acquisitions.

I proposed a similar after-the-fact solution once I realized that it was as impractical to talk about one person working 23,000 years to get rid of the files, as it was to think about hiring 23,000 people and disposing of all the paper in one year. The inspiration came one day when I read about the misery being heaped on Washington by all the roosting pigeons and crows, and realized how economical it would be to train them to carry the paper to the Potomac. After determining that these birds could be taught in a week to perch on the rail of the 14th Street Bridge and peck papers into the river at the rate of one sheet a second, I submitted the proposal in writing. But it didn't fare well during Coordination. One response spoke of the difficulties in forcing the birds from the buildings to the rails. City planners said that the number of birds involved would make the plan unworkable. All the rails of the Wilson, Chain, Key, Memorial, 14th Street, and Cabin John bridges wouldn't hold them. I responded with calculations showing that just two more bridges would do it. But the Dept. of Interior killed the idea when they brought up the pollution factor.

At least that's what I thought, and I never bothered to revive the plan. But then one day, a long time later, I was surprised to read in the *Washington Star* how somebody suggested that the building ledges be wired to shock the birds off their roosts; no mention was made of wiring the bridge rails. The clincher came though, when contruction started on two new bridges. I knew then that one day I'd see thousands of crows pecking away at the surplus files.

While I may never get the credit for the idea, I smile inwardly at the honor paid to me each time I hear a fellowcrat exclaim, "All this paperwork is for the birds."

Such physical measures will take care of the present surpluses, and the explain-it-all-the-first-time school of writing will one day control the source. But something more needs to be done about the accumulations, present and future. And you just can't ask a Bureaucrat to quit writing. Before examining some of the solutions, however, the causes behind the propensity to save should be investigated.

The first cause dawned on me when I overheard a maestrocrat tell his secretary, "Sugar, This is a CYA report. Better get it in the mill right away."

"What's 'CYA' stand for?" I asked.

"Chronicle Your Actions" he replied with a wry smile. "They used to be called Pearl Harbor Files. They're for protection."

And this is one of the fundamental lessons in Bureaucracy. One never knows which document he'll have to produce to prove:

a. That he did say, order, mean or imply something which got the office involved in a Program that was a rousing success; or

b. That he did *not* say, order, mean or imply something which got the office involved in a Program that wasted money or embarrassed the office.

So one keeps them all. Indefinitely. It's called Background.

There is another basic reason for hanging on to things. Within three days after you've thrown something away, you need it. This is common in the outside world, too. It's just more frequent in Bureaucracy because of the surprise demands for Background.

Next, it's natural for someone to keep something that has been created through extraordinarily hard work, and most of Bureaucracy's Programs fit into this category. So rather than destroy it himself, the creator files it away for an uninvolved replacement to, perhaps, discard.

Finally, there is an economic motive. Most good Bureaucrats can't bear to waste anything that is public property, so their collective conscience won't allow them to burn the old files. In fact, it's so rare that those who produce paper destroy it that administrative maestrocrats have made the act a "significant accomplishment." For example, a group in Washington issued instructions on "records disposition" which said:

"Narrative Reporting. Report all significant accomplishments such as . . . cost savings realized through the destruction of non-current records in the office or by retirement of a large volume of records to the Federal Records Center." Then it went on to tell how to fill in and file the copies of the "significant accomplishment report." A "table of equivalents for calculating cubic footage of records" was supplied so that drawer space freed could be converted to "dollar savings."

A great dent can be made in the accumulations resulting from these causes if Bureaucracy would just quit hoarding the *unnecessary* paper. This category embraces exclusively:

a. Penciled drafts kept to prove to the typist that the word was spelled correctly, punctuation was correct, or that a word was not left out.

b. First typewritten draft kept after the second draft has been prepared to verify that the second draft may have been unintentionally reworded.

c. Second draft kept for the Background on the third draft.

d. Third draft (ditto above).

e. Etc.

f. Literary copy held because some of the wording was nicely done and might be used again later.

g. Contingency copies. These are the five or ten extra copies made in case somebody was overlooked in mailing or addressing; or somebody needs some more from which to make reproductions.

The measure I propose next is revolutionary. I maintain that as long as there must be files, then let's make them more *valuable* from the standpoint of sheer volume as well as contents. That way, there won't be so much bellyaching about having to store them. This can be accomplished by using them as a standard—a criterion. Before this is dismissed as a three-martini concept, let me point out that it may have already been tried.

There has been a good bit of speculation about just how the C-5 Galaxy, the world's largest cargo plane, came to be as big as it is; *six stories high and a block or so long.* Most Air Force-philes subscribe to the reason given in the *Air Force Fact Sheet;* i.e., to "provide a vast capability for rapid deployment of both combat forces and their fighting equipment." I prefer to think that a PAPER CRITERION experiment is in progress and that it will be made known when it is proved successful.

Rumor has it that back in 1950 an Air Force general, dismayed at the mountains of proposals he had to plow through, said to his aide, "By Gawd, Alphie! I wish somebody'd build an airplane big enough to carry all the Gawdamned paper it takes to get it built! That way we'd be able to carry all we needed to!" Knowing that a general's wish is a colonel's panic, I felt that something must have come of it.

Returning to the House Committee on PO and CS, I learned that the invitations to bid on the Galaxy were 1500 pages long. The five competing contractors responded in 240,000 pages. These were reproduced in 30 copies and distributed for review to 400 people. The significant point here is the weight of the paper—35 tons! 70,000 pounds!

Now comes the matter of costs. The original estimate was about 3.2 billion dollars but the final tab amounted to 5 billion, or about 60 percent over estimate. Acting on the assumption that the size of the aircraft would be proportional to the weight of the paper, I concluded that the costs would be related to the size in the same manner. Therefore we must add 60 percent of the original weight of paper (70,000 lbs) which is 42,000; then 70,000 and 42,000 total up to 112,000 lbs. To this add 1000 lbs. for paper clips and staples and the total is 113,000 lbs. *This*

*is exactly the cargo carrying capacity of the C-5A, and is quoted
in the fact sheet describing its characteristics.*

It is not hard to envision the immense value the files will
take on as they are used as standards for larger aircraft carriers,
space stations, submarine fleets, and transports. Bureaucracy
will no longer have to fight for storage space, and fellowcrats
won't have to blush over the file drawers pregnant with their
creations. And the time will come when the old request—"Can
we get that in writing"—will be given the honored reception it
deserves.

16

THE SEA OF COORDINATION

EVERYBODY KNOWS ABOUT John Paul Jones and his famous retort, "I have just begun to fight," shouted in response to a proposal to surrender. But only a few people know of the earthy pronouncement muttered by the marine who lay injured at Jones' feet. The battle was raging. Cannon balls were toppling the rigging and grape shot raked the deck. The ship was taking water and listing dangerously; men screamed in pain midst the gunsmoke and fire. After surveying the holocaust around him, and hearing Jones' reply, the marine struggled to one elbow, looked disdainfully at the Admiral and mumbled to nobody in particular, "There's always some son-of-a-bitch who never gets the word."

His pedestrian comment, while not enshrined in the annals of raw beef heroism, is quoted a lot more often than "I have just begun to fight!" In fact, it is heard most anytime somebody who should know doesn't know and screws up a Program. To guard against this, Coordination was invented. It not only insures that everybody gets the word, but that they get to add some to it. And, indeed, the difficulties authorities have had with the Ten Commandments and the Constitution show all too clearly the consequences of not getting full Coordination. I can't help but think that had these documents been passed around so that affected agencies could have made their contributions, sin and our pursuits of happiness wouldn't carry such a long, gray look.

Without good Coordination, the chaos that dogs the System would soon catch up with it completely instead of just once in a while. And, of course, each time somebody fails to get the word, the minimum consequence is embarrassment.

For example; Senator Gaylord Nelson asked the Navy Department for information on a super secret communications network code named Sanguine. The Navy complied by sending him reproductions of news clippings. However, each one was stamped "Secret" and had to be handled accordingly. Somebody didn't get the word that public print needn't be classified.

The maximum that can happen is to inflict an inconvenience on some good fellowcrat. That is, money will be channeled down a drain other than the one intended. Programmers will have to go to the trouble of justifying (a) why, even though it went down the wrong channel, it did some good, and (b) why more money will be needed because some of the original funding went toward doing some good that hadn't been planned for. For instance; a little Coordination would have provided a tighter grip on the $35,000 spent by the Peace Corps to teach volunteers the language of the natives of Mauritius, an island in the Indian Ocean. When the imported instructors arrived, officials learned at once that the native tongue of the islanders was English. The unplanned good, of course, was that 10 Mauritians learned that English was the native tongue of the United States. And since an exchange of knowledge took place between foreigners, the $35,000 could be justified as a cultural exchange.

Many Bureaucrats look upon Coordination as a nuisance and a bulwark to Program progress. But I like to look upon it as a wide, serene sea with many mysterious ports of call. I launch my piece of the Program, then sit back and, in my mind, follow it on its peaceful journey as it goes from port to port. At each stop I know it will pick up many treasures peculiar to the port. Upon its return, these will become a wealth of new material and ideas upon which to draw when rewriting the original. And to me will accrue the credit for bringing the cargo home.

Hanging on the wall of the office of a friend at the Navy annex in Arlington, Va., was a sign saying "A collision at sea can spoil your whole day." By it I was reminded that Coordination also keeps Programs from running into each other. For instance, at the same time that the Department of Agriculture was subsidizing the tobacco farmers, HEW saw fit to spend a few thousand dollars to warn smokers of lung cancer. On a less grand scale, but more typical, was the case of a painter putting the finishing touches on a partition in a Pentagon office, when carpenters, working from the other side, began tearing it down.

Coordination, properly carried out, has other benefits. Present-day emphasis is given to the use of computerized statistics, advanced management techniques (Operations Research), and impeccable wording. It is almost impossible for only one or two Programmers to do all the research necessary to get a perfect launch the first time. Help is immediately available, though, through the added words of Coordination supplied because of the successful Bureaucrat's natural urge to:

a. Be a Good Ole Boy.

b. Be acknowledged as an authority in more than one field.

c. Check carefully somebody else's facts and figures for mistakes which, when returned corrected, will show that somebody else is just as knowledgeable about the subject as the originator.

d. Make certain that other offices have not taken over part or all of a Project, Task or Effort rightfully belonging to somebody else.

Under these stimulants, answers and responses will fill in the gaps. Exact values will replace the approximations sent out; suspected facts will come back substantiated, modified, or refuted. Wording will be changed to fit the Protective Vocabulary being applied at the time. There remains, then, only to do a little editing and rewriting.

Coordination is also an airtight way of getting other Bureaucrats, and even entire Agencies, to share the responsibilities (therefore, blame!) implicit in any proposal. If a great number of people have helped launch a Program and it should go astray, picking one or two fellowcrats as scapegoats will be very difficult.

All in all, though, Coordination is welcome most as a shield against the Fear of Unforeseen Disaster (FUD). This is the fear of being proved grotesquely wrong after a Program has been formally accepted into the System. Now, this is not fear in its classic sense; nobody's going to be jailed or tortured. Far from it; the most that can happen is a promotion and transfer. So the fear is reduced to the kind one might experience when, at a cocktail party, he rams both hands in his pockets, rears back to laugh at a joke, then can't remember whether or not his fly is zipped. This, the open-fly syndrome, keeps good Bureaucrats Coordinating long and hard to avoid being the object of ridicule. Therefore, Coordination offers security in the sense that "If I've made a mistake, somebody out there will pick it up."

Any Coordination worth its routing slip is a long-term process involving several Coordinatees: The office chief who assigns the Task of reading and commenting; the fellowcrat to whom he assigns the job; the secretary who must draft the comments and prepare the final work for dispatch; since all programs involve money, at least one person from the next higher echelon must pass on it as must three people from the budget shop, one from personnel, and one from the executive office who must see that the mechanics, security and spelling are correct. So even the most rudimentary Coordination involves nine people.

These comments are then incorporated into the first revision, and the new draft is sent around for another check for accuracy, and to show the contributing Bureaucrats that their work wasn't ignored. On this trip, only 50 percent of the original Coordinatees add their afterthoughts and correct misuses of the P.V. Sometimes sentences that are so specific as to be a closed-end commitment for some coordinatee are loosened up a little. This stage involves five more people. Thus, when the final version is dispatched as a Program, a minimum of 14 fellowcrats have had a chance to get, expand and spread the word.

Only the most experienced Maestrocrats know all the sections and offices that must be included in Coordination. Those of less experience, not being certain of the addressee's degree of interest, send the paper out marked "For Your Information." That way, if there happens to be an interest, the recipient is free to respond; otherwise he can file the paper as Background.

There is also a technique to being a good Coordinatee. It is not polite Bureaucratting to come right out and say something is wrong, ill-thought-out, impractical, or stupid. The accomplished coordinatee lives up to the GOB standard, using cautious sentences. Several benefits accrue:

a. The fellowcrat who sent the Program around will not get angry about the comments. Later when the positions are reversed, there is little likelihood of his harboring any desire to "get even."

b. There is always the chance that an unseen, powerful hand guides the Program. One should take care not to antagonize such a power by being too coarse in specifying the deficiencies.

c. No matter how careful one may be in reviewing the proposed Program, there remains the nagging doubt that something may be wrong in the Coordination comments themselves. This leads to Secondary Fear of Unforseen Disaster (SFUD) and again, the open-fly syndrome.

Examples of good Coordination and the products thereof can be seen by selecting at random from the hundreds of thousands that are hidden away in the files. But they are "inside" and to grasp the significance of the wording, one should really be part of it. Since this won't be possible for everybody until B-Day, I've selected an example which all will understand.

Let us suppose that President Lincoln's speech writers had Coordinated the Gettysburg Address with the Departments of State and Defense, with a "For Your Information" to the Department of Health, Education, and Welfare. It would begin with a memo thus:

The attached address is submitted for review and comment

as necessary. Reply should reach this office not later than 19 May 1863.

"Fourscore and seven years ago our fathers brought forth on this continent, a new nation, conceived in liberty and dedicated to the proposition that all men are created equal. Now we are engaged in a great civil war, testing . . . " Etc. Etc.

Comments would be sent back as follows:

State Department: It is our considered opinion that the statement as it stands in the opening sentence could possibly subject our foreign policy to criticism. It is believed that the entire continent was not "brought forth," just parts of it. Unless Canada and Mexico are cited specifically as exclusions to the area referenced, world opinion may hold that we have imperialisticized our policies.

Department of Defense: First sentence: Experts, after reassuring themselves through statistical and historical research, believe that "brought forth" minimizes the role of the military establishment. Discussion with the Army and Navy indicated unanimously that we should emphasize to a greater degree the successful application of arms as an instrument of national policy. We believe also that the use of the expression "civil war" is somewhat overstating the present issue. The conflict is not such that the entire population is actively involved and hence could be held to be, and better termed, a *limited action.*

Department of Health, Education and Welfare: Although not directly in the chain of command for comments, we believe our Programs and positions are such that they could be jeopardized were we to neglect asking that our opinions and comments be considered. We believe that "our fathers" should be re-examined as to fitness of expression. Many of those engaged in the circa '76 conflict were not fathers. In many cases, those who were fathers were not necessarily the fathers of those to whom the address is to be made. Consequently we believe that some may take offense at having been discriminated against because all the credit would go to those who did have fathers involved. In other instances, pacifist elements have voiced objections to their forebearer's participation and have demonstrated in front of the White House by burning their DAR cards. We feel also the "fourscore and seven" is a somewhat snobbish expression for use at a battle field. Moreover, in the matter of "men" being equal; we believe firmly that in the interest of the Women's Liberation Movement, "women" should be mentioned specifically. However, if the word women is to be used, we urge that "proposition" be stricken from the text. There should be no implication that any of the equal women referred to were ever propositioned.

And so it would go, down through the address until the entire text had been analyzed word for word, rewritten to accommodate the suggestions, and Coordinated again. Finally, the opening sentence of the Gettysburg Address would be delivered as:

"About 87 years ago, the military establishment supported by certain select civilian elements engaged in a conflict designed to repel British aggression. In so doing, imperialistic advances were forestalled, and we were brought into a position such that acceptable control could be exercised over the land area between Canada and Mexico to the north and south, respectively, and bounded by the Atlantic and Pacific Oceans on the east and west respectively. Military and subsequent civilian administrations were such that de jure and de facto discrimination was, to a large extent, discontinued. And now we are, by definition, engaged in a limited action to enable a comprehensive determination as to whether or not . . . " etc.

It becomes patently clear that had Mr. Lincoln appreciated

the value of Coordination, he would have been entirely too busy to have spent his time at the theatre. He'd have been home at the White House putting together future masterpieces.

17
ABUSES

THE LAST CHAPTER showed how Coordination is used to let fellowcrats know what's coming, to gather enough facts and opinions to ward off mistakes, to maintain the GOB image by telling a fellowcrat what you're going to do to him, then letting him tell you how to do it. But there are three types of abuses.

l. The Uncommitted Involvement or the Committed Uninvolvement. Here responses to Coordination requests are worded to give the impression of careful review, but neither involve, nor not involve the responding office. Protected thus, the commenting Bureaucrat can sift through the wording and corner a little credit should the Program prove to be a fast burner. On the other hand, he is in an "I told you so" stance should there be justification for the open-fly syndrome.

I confess that I have used this technique as the following response, from my missiles and space days at Vandenberg AFB, shows. It is quoted only so the unpracticed can catch a little of the flavor.

"This office is of the strong opinion that there is considerable merit to an approach something like this, although care must be taken in making sure that there are no loose ends. It is stressed that its value will be as stated only if there is a certainty that this can be done without any hidden costs cropping up later, and that the results will be totally beneficial."

Observe the two salient characteristics: To pick out any specific commitment, non-commitment, involvement or non-involvement would be like nailing a custard pie to the wall. And it differs from the Universal Response because it avoids three-ply weight factors, making it more straightforward.

2. *The "Play It Again, Sam" Response.* In this case the Coordinatee creates the impression that he's looked into all the minute cracks and corners of the Program, and that he agrees completely. This is accomplished by *explaining back* to the originator exactly what it was he said in the first place. A thesaurus and some paraphrasing are all the respondee needs to insure a sizable chunk of credit on a surefire Program.

3. *The Quickie.* If a Program is suspect or there are complications that would be detected under routine Coordination, the unscrupulous Coordinatee may try to fast-shuffle his Program through, e.g., "Can you rush this through? It's gotta be done *yesterday!* Really a hot one! I sure would appreciate it if I could get your chop right after lunch or the first thing in the morning at the latest."

When thus approached, remember: the closer the request is to lunch hour, or the close of the work day, the more likely there is to be a fast one buried somewhere in the bulk, and the closer should be the scrutiny to which the Program is subjected.

These are but venial sins. Nonetheless the conscientious Bureaucrat should make a habit of using them. And if caught in such a Coordination crack, he should immediately return the paper to the originating office and ask for more information, or clarification. This will buy time until one can find out what to do, or delay action until the responsibility for the Coordination can be passed to some other office.

18

THE LANCE AND WINDMILL SYNDROME

THE NEWCOMER TO Bureaucracy, upon seeing the office furniture stacked in the hall, may get the impression that the System's physical plant is in a constant state of upheaval. However, it is under control and no cause for concern.

About every 13 to 17 months, fellowcrats and entire offices are beset by the Lance and Windmill Syndrome, characterized by listlessness, long sighs of resignation, a sense of futility, and, of course, halls full of desks, chairs, trash baskets, etc. During these times it seems that no matter how hard one strives, the Projects and Programs will never get through being reviewed and revised. Papers believed to be masterpieces of meticulous phrasing and incontestable justification come back bearing a hastily scribbled margin note, "I think you should say 'possible' here instead of 'probable'." The history major up the line responds with, "This didn't work too well when we tried it 13 years ago." The empire builder imposes an impossible load with his, "This is OK but we should consider expanding it so we can absorb the other two offices and bring them under one head. Cuts out duplication of effort."

Other Coordination comments, once a source of help, are looked upon as the mutterings of obstructionists who are embalmed in the status quo. Or the victim sees them as:

a. A refusal to take on any more work or a different kind of work.

b. A stall.

c. A put-down to keep one from looking too good too soon.

The syndrome, if not recognized in time, pushes one into a paranoid state. It creeps up quietly until it rests full blown on the victim who reacts by:

a. Shunting: i.e., not doing all the Coordination necessary.

b. Stopping work on all Tasks that involve anybody outside the originating office.

c. Talking fondly of a transfer to another Agency or office.

d. Threatening to go to work for industry.

e. A combination of the above.

So, being aware of the syndrome, I realize that it will go away only after I accomplish something that has short term, tangible results. So, I assemble my staff and we rearrange the furniture.

The new position of each piece is first planned in detail using a scaled floor plan and scaled cut-outs, these representing the office furniture. Once things are worked out on paper, the actual shift begins. Most of the larger pieces are put in the hall so there is room to move around. While exposed, the backs and sides of the filing cabinets and desks, the undersides of the chairs, and the exposed walls are wiped clean of coffee streaks, cobwebs and dust. The glass desk covers are removed and polished on both sides. The things that were underneath—pictures, slogans, telephone numbers, amusing cards, cartoons, notices, organizational charts, and reminders are brought up to date and rearranged. The telephones are wiped clean to such an extent that a damp rag on the end of a letter opener is used to wipe the dust from under the dial. All the papers and paraphernalia are taken from the desk drawers, which are dumped, thumped and ragswiped to get out the bent paper clips and old coffee cake crumbs.

The rearrangement tapers off by mid-afternoon. Everybody sits back contentedly surveying the new surroundings, determined to make a start that is as clean as the office. But we'll start tomorrow; that way, the day will be fresh, too. The heaped "IN" basket no longer seems to be such a challenge. We are once more at peace with ourselves.

And later in the days and weeks and months that follow as we stroll to the coffee shop, or visit other Agencies and Bureaus, it will be comforting to see the flurry of activity here and there as other offices find their respective ways to peace and satisfaction by rearranging the furniture.

Once in awhile when we see a new building rising or another addition being built, we marvel and speculate among ourselves at the awesome levels of Bureaucracy, and how vast the Sea of Coordination must be to demand such stupendous measures to dispel their Lance and Windmill Syndrome.

19

MONEY
OF
UNSPECIFIED
DENOMINATION (MUD)

IN SPITE OF EVIDENCE to the contrary, the System *isn't* free. There are dollars that are attached and because of this, many tyrocrats impede Program progress by their reluctance to spend the huge sums necessary to finalize a Program. So inhibiting, sometimes, is this feeling that by the time the money is requested, the Project for which it is intended is no longer required.

However, spending will come naturally and easily once it is understood that there are really *two entirely different kinds of legal tender in use by the System!* One counts; one doesn't.

The first type of money is the day-to-day or "real" kind that everybody uses to pay the bills. This type is rare, and always in short supply when needed most.

The other type is the tender used for Bureaucratting; i.e., Money of Unspecified Denomination, or MUD.

MUD is produced by a special process. Real money is sent to governments in the form of taxes and is immediately machine processed to remove all the amount marks from both sides. Then when Bureaucracy wants to buy something, the proper number of blanks are selected and appropriate amount marks reinserted until there is enough to cover costs and still keep the pile to a manageable size. Since there are enormous amounts involved, the basic counting unit is the million, which Bureaucracy calls a *megabuck*. Below one megabuck, in the petty cash range, the unit is the *thou* or the *K*.

Recently there has been a trend toward costing and expensing in terms of the height of the Washington Monument. It was started in the outside world when an insurance company advertised, "If the $6,000,000 paid out in benefits were changed to silver dollars, the stack would reach 100 times as high as the Washington Monument." In anticipation of the System adopting this unit, I have prepared a handy conversion table. (WM = Washington Monument.)

$6,000,000 = 6 megabucks = 100 WM
$3,000,000 = 3 megabucks = 50 WM
$1,000,000 = 1 megabuck = 16.6 WM
    $60,000 = 60 thou or 60 K = 1 WM

Other factions talk of converting costs to one dollar bills, laying them end-to-end and expensing in terms of number of times around the equator, or to the moon and back, but I advocate the WM scale because it is easier to visualize.

Once the money is put through the marks remover, any connection it had with its original owner is severed. With the last trace of value removed, and all pecuniary restraints with it, the Bureaucrat is free to function with maximum efficiency. That is, he can charge ahead to the extent that he is not delayed by a mispricked conscience or the tight-fistedness associated with "real" money.

For example, the head of a large government agency sent an aide to see to the printing of a sizable Report. In the interest of haste, it was taken to a private firm with the request that it be finished "by Friday morning. We need it for distribution." The printer pointed out some difficulties and a number of needed corrections, and told the aide that it couldn't be finished until the following Monday without spending a fortune for overtime. The aide, being totally uninhibited, replied, "To hell with the expense. The boss wants this on Friday, and money is no object!" Thanks to the aide's decision, the report—exploring the methods whereby the Agency could save money—was available for study on Friday as planned.

The advantages of effortless spending are clear and the MUD theory can be substantiated to promote it. A piece of hard evidence became available in the early 1960s when the United States wanted to borrow 500 megabucks from the International Monetary Fund to strengthen the dollar which was under heavy attack by foreign interests. The loan was approved, of course, since we are the heaviest contributor to the IMF. And were it not for the two different types of money, we would have been in the impossible position of borrowing our own money.

20
"I DON'T KNOW"

"I DON'T KNOW" are the three most abhorred words in Bureaucracy. The stigma was originally attached eons ago when the System was building its first pyramids. I discovered this fact when studying some circa-3000 B.C. writings taken from the tomb of an Egyptian high priest. In a photograph of some hieroglyphics on a chamber wall, I noted the drawing of a man standing blank-eyed, arms partially outstretched with palms up, and shoulders in the shrug position (below).*

*Sketch made from photo in *Horizon Book of Lost Worlds,* American Heritage Pub. Co. N.Y., Page 45.

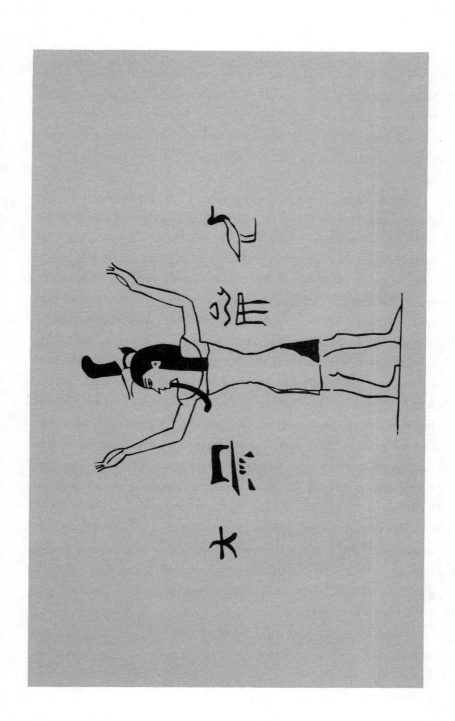

Although Egyptologists may disagree with me, I am certain that the figure was that of a middle-management official, probably a branch or division chief. I deduce this from what appears to be his badge of office, the chicken feather head-piece. (This is undoubtedly the origin of the modern day method of referring to supervisors as "He's a chicken," or more simply, "He's chicken!")

Only the principal hieroglyphics are reproduced in the sketch, but they tell the story. One day a bulge appeared in the ceiling of one of the tomb's inner chambers. An inspector (depicted as small Chinese-like character at left) asked the supervisor what to do about it. The official, only recently transferred from the Secret Passages branch, shrugged his shoulders and said, "I don't know." At that instant the bulge erupted and a gigantic stone fell from the ceiling on to the supervisor, making him one with the floor. The crashing block and the devastation it wrought are represented by the splashy characters just to the left of the chief. The hieroglyphics at right represent his departing soul wafting upward; the chicken at far right indicates that the badge of office awaits a replacement. The tragedy is still commemorated whenever one Bureaucrat says to another; "He'd better have the answer, or he'll think the roof fell in on him."

In contemporary Bureaucracy, "I don't know" is only permissible in one's own office when no decisions are being made, and no official information is being passed. Clearly, it's no disgrace to tell a fellowcrat "I don't know" if he asks the time and your watch is broken.

But such a confession blurted out during the question-and-answer sessions that follow briefings exposes gaps in knowledge. Fortunately, there are several simple ways to avoid ever having to say "I don't know."

Bud Nipping: The first questions are apt to be fired at you during the course of the presentation. The probability of this happening can be reduced by bud nipping. That is, ask the group at the very beginning to withhold their questions until the talk is finished. If the request is ignored, tell the questioner that you've anticipated his question and will answer it later in the talk. Most likely, it will be forgotten by the time you are concluding your remarks.

Coffee, Tea or John Technique: The highest hurdle comes at the conclusion of the talk. The lights come on and the view-graph machine is turned off. Several feisty juniors, anxious to impress people, will be squirming in their seats waiting to pounce on some of the not-too-firm points you hoped would glide by unnoticed. So before you acknowledge any of the faces that are screwed anxiously into the I-have-a-question-configuration, look directly at the most important person present (MIPP), and while wiping your brow with your handkerchief, ask him if he'd like to take a coffee break. Immediately look past him and around the room wearing a questioning expression. This will remind him that even if he doesn't want (need) one, there may be others who do. Out of thoughtfulness he'll agree to the break. If you sense that getting the point across will be difficult, move from behind the table or podium, squirm a little or stand first on one foot and then the other, then ask directly, or say something like, "We've been at this for quite a while now. Would you like to unwind a little? I know I would."

These methods may not always work, so if you want to play it safe, I recommend that natural inclinations be stimulated. It's a cinch that some of the members drank something last night, at the preceding meal or previous break. You can remind them of it by pouring yourself a glass of water. Do so by holding the carafe about a foot above the glass and let the water trickle suggestively into it. After you've drunk deeply a couple of times, ask about the break.

Once the intermission is at hand, the golden door is open. During this period of relief make yourself available for questions. The anxious inquisitors will accost you at once and you can thrash the problems out quietly and semi-privately. If conditions are right, a Universal Response will be in order. Then, during the last few minutes, talk with the MIPP and steer the conversation to something he likes to talk about, or tell him something you know he'll be delighted to hear. These things consume time and establish a camaraderie heightening the GOB instinct to avoid embarrassing you by asking awkward questions.

The longer you can keep them out of their seats, the better. It sets a more convincing stage when you tell them that you've overshot your schedule and must leave at once for another appointment. Excuse yourself by saying that any questions can be written on scratch paper and dropped off with your secretary, and that you'll have the answer typed up and delivered. It is most improbable that this will ever happen. And even if it does, you'll not have to say "I don't know."

Shill Method: There are two versions of this. The first calls for close timing. Have your secretary or some other trustworthy agent interrupt the briefing at some point very close to the conclusion. They should do so by slipping up quietly and handing you a folded slip of paper which you unfold and read at once. Leave immediately, forgetting to take your notes and slides.

The second approach is less dramatic, but as effective. Arm a fellowcrat with a couple of questions and plant him in the audience. Acknowledge his first, and gear your answers to fill the remaining time.

Flood-Gate Method: If, in spite of all your efforts, the

inquisition proceeds, respond to the question for which you have no answer by giving an answer to a related one, and for which you were prepared but not asked. Make a good show of it. Clasp your hands behind your back and look at the floor for a while as though framing the words. This will give a moment or two to overcome the shock and to regain your composure. Then give forth with a long, involved dissertation, well countersunk, and delivered with much sincerity. The flood-gate method will dampen any further enthusiasm for asking questions, if for no other reason than that the listeners are hesitant about getting you started again.

If you are unable to grab on to a thread which will relate the answer to the question, ask that it be repeated. It will not be asked in the same form, but will be paraphrased either because the inquisitor thinks he hasn't made himself clear, or he's forgotten exactly what it was he asked. You now have two sets of leads from which a tie-in can be found. Once grasped, resort to a UR with extemporaneous paraphrasing to make it relevant. It will be rare that you'll be told you haven't answered the question. The questioner will believe that you did answer it and he just didn't understand. And he may feel that some of the others understood it and he won't want to appear stupid.

21

"I.I.D.I.F.Y.I.G.T.D.I.F.E."

WHEN I WORKED for the Defense Intelligence Agency, each morning I would stand in line for the security badge that would admit me to the sanctuary behind the vault-like doors where the supersecrets were. One morning I found myself shuffling along behind a young secretary who'd been on maternity leave. In her arms was a month-old infant, her son, whom she'd brought with her to be admired by co-workers as she was being brought up to date prior to returning to work. Cheerfully she asked the guard for her pass. He pulled the laminated card from the rack and started to hand it to her. Then he stopped short. "What about the baby?" he asked. "Everybody—visitors too—gotta have a pass."

A confrontation arose as the girl became indignant. She didn't get the guard's point when he told her that he didn't make the rules, he just enforced them. She played on his sympathies, cunningly dropping such irrationalities as " . . . only a month old" and " . . . just a baby," etc. She persisted in her arguments to get in the Building until the guard unsheathed Bureaucracy's most potent special privilege stopper: "If I do it for you, I gotta do it for everybody."

Bravo!

It stopped her cold and she retreated embarrassed and ashamed.

The effectiveness of the squelcher herein after referred to as I.I.D.I.F.Y.I.G.T.D.I.F.E., lies in the visions it provokes in the minds of the victims. The young secretary was forced to visualize thousands of young secretary-mothers, month-old babes in arms, all converging on the hapless guard, screaming, clamoring and clawing to be admitted to the security area without passes for their infants.

While the squelcher puts the victim on the defensive and makes him feel ashamed, he must remember that he can't afford to knock points off his Good Ole Boy index. Still, he must remind the requestor that the rule comes first and that behind one exception lies a hundred thousand more.

All this can be accomplished quite safely by emphasizing certain words according to status of the individual and conditions under which the rule is to be applied.

Below are listed the circumstances, with the initial in the abbreviation underlined to show where emphasis should be placed. I recommend that the tyrocrat memorize this list without further delay:

1. I I D I F __Y__ I G T D I F E : You outrank the requestor.

2. I I D I F Y I G T D I F __E__ : Requestor outranks you.

3. I I D I F __Y__ I G T D I F __E__ : Equal rank.

4. I I D I F Y I GT D I F E : A girl requestor. Or perhaps someone about whom you're not sure, or whom you suspect might be able to cause you trouble.

5. __I I D I F Y I G T D I F E__ : Someone you know can't do anything to or for you.

6. #@**!◌& I I D I F Y % $ # % I G T D I F E # $ † $ ** !?†: Someone with whom you want to get even, don't like, and know that he can't do anything for you.

7. "SURE. I'll take care of it for you soon as I'm through here. But don't tell anybody because, then, I I D I F Y I G T D I F E : A close friend, or someone to whom you owe a favor, or from whom you intend to ask a favor.

Once again, practice will give the tyrocrat a jump on experience. Endless arguments and embarrassments will be shunted, and fellowcrats and entire offices will be spared the extra work that may occur were precedents set by giving in to special requests.

22

DELUSION DEPTHS

(Part 1 of a Trilogy on Accolades)

I'VE BEEN TOLD that once in a while a sightseer along the Potomac, late in the evening, may happen upon one of Bureaucracy's more tragic dramas. As the tale goes, a solitary figure can be seen walking with great deliberateness to a spur of land that juts into the confluence of the Potomac and Anacostia rivers. The guide books call this "Haines Point"; but wise old maestrocrats nod their heads knowingly and call it "Delusion Depths."

The shadowy form will pause at the water's edge, and with a flourish remove a couple of sheets of typewritten paper from his inside pocket. The papers are well worn and dog-eared, having been read and re-read. Ceremoniously he'll unfold them and by the remaining light, read and re-read them some more. Then, head high, he'll step out full stride onto the water!

Thrashing arms! Churning water! Shouts for help rend the quiet hours as another good tyrocrat tragically tries to cross that mighty river without using the bridge. Alas, he believed what was written of him in his performance rating.

I Shudder.

Unfortunately no amount of warning will dissuade the tyrocrat from taking at face value all of the good things that have been written of him in Bureaucracy's annual report card— the effectiveness report or performance rating.

I realize that the human side of Bureaucracy compels one to be almost as quick to believe the best about one's self as to believe the best about another. So I don't say "Don't! Please don't." Still, I'm obliged to say something; therefore I say to the tyrocrat, "Learn to Swim!"

Sadly, many of these efficiency ratings are no more than placebos. To illustrate, I've concocted a Mr. Flubton, and have given him an effectiveness report made up of phrasing taken from genuine accounts. What actually happened appears in ordinary type; what was communicated to experienced Bureaucrats and maestrocrats follows in italics.

NARRATIVE ACCOUNT:

"Mr. Flubton has been chief of our small but busy records section for ten years. *(Mr. Flubton doesn't have a very important job and he has not been promotional material.)* Over the past year as always before, he has applied himself with extraordinary diligence, enhancing the general efficiency of the office to such an extent that it has not been necessary to ask for additional help in spite of the usual workload and overtime accrued by his section. *(This year just like all the rest, he's had to do a lot of unnecessary work himself, and call for a good bit*

120

of staff overtime just to keep up.) In his daily tasks he devotes a considerable amount of time to every detail no matter how seemingly inconsequential. He is skillful at encouraging initiative, permitting others to handle the less subtle points at issue. *(By spending too much time on trivia, all the important things are left for somebody else to do.)* Being most receptive to friendly criticisms, no time is wasted in incorporating suggestions into his work even though it means sacrificing many hours to extra effort while re-doing the job to perfection. *(His work has many mistakes in it and must be done over repeatedly before it is acceptable.)* Even so, he is extremely conscientious in his desire to meet a deadline, and often carries projects personally through channels, insuring the attention of superiors and other supervisors. *(Usually late with his projects, he panics and rushes them through channels himself, inconveniencing everybody.)* Mr. Flubton has demonstrated with increasing frequency lately, that he is capable of putting out a constant amount of work with less personal attention. Under this method of operation he has made his staff particularly adept at acting on their own. *(Flubton goofs off a good bit of the time. It doesn't matter though, because usually his staff gets the decisions without him.)* I find that this man is completely satisfactory as an employee who really gets the job done. I support any means taken to insure that this fine worker is retained in his present position. *(I may not be able to get a replacement, and since he doesn't get me in any real trouble and can ordinarily do the minimum expected, I'll keep him. But don't promote him this year either.)"*

After all the emphasis that has been spent in disproving the idea that Bureaucracy is annealed in negativism, the above example must seem out of context. But it's not, for it demonstrates how to shine a positive light on a negative performance.

23

MEDALS AND CITATIONS: ANOTHER PATH TO THE RIVER

(Part 2 of a Trilogy on Accolades)

BELIEVING WHAT IS written to justify one's special award or medal can get one just as wet as believing his performance rating.

Recently it has become the vogue to bestow a special award whenever possible, and nearly any benchmark will suffice for cause, e.g.:

a. Finalizing a "short-term" project that has been a thorn in the office's side for up to 18 months.

b. Finalization of a long-term project (18 months to four years) about which an entirely new organization has been built.

c. Transferring after four or more years in one office

during which daily tasks were performed with minimum bitch-ing and without much inconvenience to others.

d. Retirement.

For example, in late 1966 a medal was awarded to a Wash-ington, D.C. Bureaucrat of long and good standing for a type "a" Task (see above). The citation described him as a supervisor "who between July 1963 and December 1964" was engaged in solving battlefield lighting problems and who succeeded by "turning night into day."

Such heady brew once was reserved for maestrocrats, and the tyrocrat was expected to look on and be inspired. House organs were filled with stories and photos of seasoned Bureau-crats honoring other seasoned Bureaucrats in a daisy chain of tributes. It was difficult to find a warm-bodied civil servant who'd worked his way up to a wooden desk, without being presented with at least one such award. But that was long ago when things done by tyrocrats were ignored because it was too much trouble to write them up.

Now good work is being sought out and the significance attached to accomplishments is being revised upward. At the same time the concept of accomplishment is being revised downward to a more real level.

Take the case of an Air Force Lieutenant who was stationed at Hancock Field, New York. He was awarded the Air Force Commendation Medal for designing and building a swimming pool for the Officer's club. The citation concluded by citing his "unselfish devotion of time and energy above and beyond the line of duty."

There appears to be the unexpressed understanding that a competition exists among chiefs to see who can get the most and highest awards for their people. In many cases superiors are looking upon the Tasks assigned them as "certificate only," "one-medal" or "two-medal," etc. In fact, more and more often now, one hears the enthusiastic assertion, "My God! Somebody ought to get a medal for *that* one."

Bureaucracy recognizes that it is impossible to perform a job for two decades without doing something spectacular. Bureaucracy also recognizes that such spectacular performances might be overlooked. To insure that this does not happen, the Air Force Systems Command has developed the following form letter that is presented on the last day of duty:

Dear Colonel Doe

On behalf of the United States Air Force and those of us with whom you have been associated, I would like to express sincere gratitude and appreciation for your more than _____ years of loyal and dedicated service.

I am sure you must feel a great sense of personal satisfaction from the many contributions you have made during these years of service. This sense of achievement is justifiable, for the completion of your active military career on _____ marks the end of a distinctive military service to your country. Our strength and continued protection of the free world depends on individuals like you who are willing to devote themselves to a demanding career that involves many personal sacrifices and ever-increasing responsibilities in the growth and development of aerospace power.

As ____(list job title)____, you have contributed significantly to the success of our mission. Please accept my congratulations for a job well done. I wish you continued success in all your endeavors and many years of happiness in your well-earned retirement ahead.

Sincerely

(Signature block, rank and title.)

NOTE: Any personal comments the Director feels are appropriate should be included in the letter. A letter with a personal touch will be appreciated more than a 'form letter.'

24

THE POWER OF SUGGESTION

(Part 3 of a
Trilogy on Accolades)

AFTER FOOD AND SEX, man's next greatest urge is to tell the other fellow how to do his job better. Bureaucracy, quick to sense this, introduced it into the System as "The Suggestion Program." Throughout the Agencies one now finds large motivating posters urging employees to "EARN BIG MONEY! SUGGEST!"

Rewards vary. Sometimes—most of the time, actually— they amount to $25 or $50 and a nice letter. Other times, the System laughs out loud and rewards the suggester out of something more than petty cash. These are rare and the ideas that earn them are the kind that effect, even rock, all Systemdom. For example: an employee of the Army's Adjutant General's Office was given $1400 and a certificate for suggesting that the military mail, then being carried overseas by air, be moved by surface transportation. Savings realized were calculated to be one megabuck!

There are two routes to success. The first leads to money; the second leads to money and acclaim. And whereas the $25 or $50 won't do much today, the acclaim will. The approach to each is straightforward enough. Invariably one will find his program being held up somewhere in the System because of a technicality. After the delay has drifted long enough to be respectable, the delayee sacrifices just enough of his Good Ole Boy index to find out what the cause is. Once he determines how the delaying office does what it does to his Program, he mentally figures a way around it. This, of course, is immediately seen as an improvement. Shortly thereafter the delayee will explain his problem to anybody that will listen and conclude with, "I don't see why those guys down there don't . . . etc." When this stage is reached, one is ready to reach for the suggestion form.

Fill it out by describing the way things are being done, and show how much it costs. In another space describe the improved method and show how little it costs. Subtract, and multiply by however many Offices, Agencies and Bureaus, etc., use or could use it. This will be the total savings and the figure upon which the reward and letter will be based.

Once it is on its way through channels, there's only to wait the three or four months it takes to work its way through the evaluation panels. Sometimes, money will be forthcoming; but one may, at the least, expect a note thanking him for participating even though the idea couldn't be incorporated.

To cash in on the acclaim, then, one must see that the idea, accepted or not, becomes a part of the performance ratings substantiating the ratee's skill at "management improvement methods." Two or three suggestions over a 12-month period can provide most of the bulk needed to get a "river-edge" report. All of which leads to promotion, pay raises, and a soft spot in the supervisor's heart because he doesn't have to sit down and grope for the words and expressions required to produce the "walk-on-water" rating.

There is another simple but more effective way to garner the accolades that float in on the Suggestion Form.

To begin ascertain which is the oldest of the office procedures now being used. If it is more than three years old, go back into the files and find the suggestion that put it into practice. Using a fresh suggestion form, interchange the old way with the new way descriptions, add in the inflation factor, and drop into the nearest Suggestion Box. Eventually, the check and smiling letter will arrive, a good performance report will be launched, and if fortunate, one might even receive special recognition at a little presentation ceremony. And all for an old, used idea brought back to life at the proper moment.

I encourage the tyrocrat to get started at once, using whatever approach suits his drives. He might want to show how much could be saved by flying military mail overseas instead of moving it by sea.

Whenever possible, it is always best to learn the details of how other offices do their work, think of an improvement (or find one in the files), or just an alternative way of doing something, and *suggest*. When the award for such a coup is made and advertised in the Bureau organ, the fact that the idea applied to another office originally will keep the sour grapes group from whispering that the awardee is being paid extra for what he's supposed to be doing in the first place. Perhaps.

25

RITUAL OF PRESENTATION (ROP)

NOWADAYS ONE SELDOM needs to wait until retirement to receive a long overdue award. Tyrocrats and maestrocrats alike stand constantly at the threshold of special recognition, and the door opens readily and often. It is essential, then, that the potential recipients be thoroughly familiar with the Ritual of Presentation (ROP). Here, too, there is considerable physical danger connected with the ceremony.

The ROP will take place before a small audience of fellow-crats each of whom has either already received an award or two, or has a nomination pending. The principals stand face to face on a small stage or dais, profiles to a photographer; awarder is to the left, awardee to the right. Beyond this, there are a number of uncomfortable moments to be anticipated.

The first one comes as an aide reads the narrative of accomplishments upon which the award is based. While this is going on, and it always seems to take a very long time, there is nothing to do but stand still and listen. During this period the awardee should try very hard to keep from grinning and shuffling self-consciously from one foot to another. This is most difficult because words cannot convey the uneasiness and extreme discomfort felt, when—completely exposed—one has to listen to a "walk-on-water" account of his own work, provided, of course, it is recognized as such. I know of cases where the awardee, caught thus unaware, looked around anxiously to see if there wasn't somebody else on the platform with him.

Therefore I recommend that the awardee think hard about bringing to fruition the seeds sown during a current courtship, or indiscretion, as the case may be. The facial expression, if no more than one of eager anticipation or of tired satisfaction, is far more appropriate than an unfelt, embarrassed smile.

The next critical moment is one which, if not watched, can degenerate into laughter-punctuated slapstick. It is the occasion of presenting the certificate.

The script calls for the awardee to extend his left hand diagonally upward and across in front of the awarder, timing it so as to be near mid-chest in time to receive the certificate which is arriving in the awarder's left hand. It is to be received in billboard position print to audience, to insure that it will not show up in the picture as a hairline edge. Otherwise the principals will appear to be awkwardly poking at one another, or speaking Italian.

At the same time the awardee's *right* hand should be proffered elbow at waist level to shake the *right* hand of the awarder, who, remember, may be concentrating on keeping the certificate straight, and worrying about it being clutched in a nervous spasm and crumpled. Once all around contact has been made, the awarder looks fondly at the awardee who in turn looks at the certificate, making sure his face is arranged in the proper expression. When all is in order, the pose is held through the photo phase.

A minor distraction will arise here when the flash bulb fails to go off. In this case, the awardee should go back to thinking about sex until the photographer gets squared away. When the flash does go off, it's the signal to step back and leave the dais.

I warn here that no matter how nervous one may be when stepping onto the platform, one must note and remember exactly where the edge of the stage is. A false, unknowing step backward has spoiled many an otherwise dignified proceeding.

The real trouble begins, however, if at the outset there is a mix-up in the certificate-intercept, hand-shake modes. All too often the unstudied, anxious reaction of the awardee is to reach for the certificate with the *right* hand instead of the left. If this happens, the awarder, conditioned to making presentations, sees the right hand in action and is reflexed into the hand-shake mode in advance of presenting the certificate. The awardee, catching himself in mid-thrust, withdraws his right hand from the intercept mission and recycles it to the hand-shake position. Instantly, upon missing the rendezvous by a split-second, the awardee shoots his hand back to the certificate position. The awarder, after having given brief chase, by now is further upset by seeing the hand he's supposed to shake waiting at chin level for the paper. He recovers quickly enough to dispatch the certificate once more. The photographer just waiting for a glimpse of the broadside, catches one and takes the picture. The flash of the bulb brings the action to a halt. Adversaries step back, shake and present in a by-the-numbers tempo. The awardee should step quickly off the dais and allow the awarder to brace himself for the next recipient.

At one time, the military began the proceedings with a salute by the awardee, to be returned by the awarder. However, this, on top of the certificate reach and hand-shake, had near tragic results. Nervous, excitable subordinates often panicked and nearly felled the awarder with an unintentional karate chop. It has since been discontinued.

Clearly, all this can be avoided with a little practice. Using wife or friend, go over the sequence of action until it is automatic.

Of course, if the awarder (or awardee) happens to be left handed, there is a statistically proven 78 percent chance that the hand-shake mix-up will occur and be more severe than an unpracticed case. Physical violence might be done. The awardee, if so embroiled, should take up a defensive position at once, and await the photographer's welcome flash.

26
TO ERR IS
BUREAUCRACY, TOO

NOT LONG AGO, House Commerce Committee legislation aimed at Federal control of "pep pills" and other such stimulants evoked this enthusiastic vote of confidence from a drug industry representative: "The way the legislation is worded and the way those officious bureaucrats at FDA (Food and Drug Administration) work, they'll be inquiring into every sale of drugs subject to misuse, and that takes in nearly everything we sell."

There is no question that only the utmost confidence in the System could prompt such testimonials to Bureaucracy's thoroughness. And for a long time, the System did all it could to play down the mistakes made, seen and understood by fellowcrats. It was not uncommon to see really lousy work receive an overdose of praise.

But all this was back when everything possible was done to maintain the System's perfectionist image. However, the image went too far and the outside world stood as much in awe of Bureaucracy's perfection as it did of computers, and a Pauper-before-the-Prince complex developed. People were afraid to approach the System. And they thought it indifferent to their needs.

The Air Force was the first to admit openly that Bureaucracy was just as error-ridden as the outside world. It did so when it launched a Program called "ZERO DEFECTS." Its purpose was to encourage everybody to attack the costly "do it over again" by doing it right the first time, that is, to produce work that has "zero defects."

The Program was inaugurated at Wright Patterson Air Force Base one crisp winter morning several years ago. Slogans appeared festooned with acronyms: "Personal Responsibility in Daily Effort"—PRIDE, and "Value in Performance Through Very Important People"—VIP VIP, were among those calculated to show the seriousness of the undertaking. Six thousand people were assembled in the University of Dayton fieldhouse, and heard personages including Generals, Governors, and Congressmen voice their support.

Attending also was the Imp of Perversity.

The audience was unable to see a scheduled movie because the houselights couldn't be turned off, the switch having broken. Toward the end of the movie, the lights finally went off, but couldn't be turned on again, the switch being equally obstinate in both positions. So the principal speaker referred to his notes with the aid of a miner's lamp. Finally, a mix-up in traffic flow caused a two thousand car traffic jam which spilled over into the neighboring suburbs.

In retrospect, the Air Force concluded that people would

understand that producing results with "ZERO DEFECTS" would not be an overnight job.

Word of the Air Force's approach and its possibilities soon got around and many parts of Bureaucracy picked up the theme. Note pads and memo blanks bore a "ZD" watermark; billboards, wall posters, and letterheads sloganed their pleas for perfection. I think though, that I was impressed most with Arlington Hall Station's contribution. Spaced across the lush green lawn well inside the main gate were eleven individual 2-foot square signboards standing neatly at attention, spelling out boldly:

And soon, others outside the Federal Bureaucracy began to publicly acknowledge mistakes to impress upon people that the System is "just one of the folks after all." Fellowcrats in the Virginia Road Commission tried it on Rt. 250 where a sign pointing to the town of Staunton was spelled "Stanuton." Officials thought it didn't matter since the town's name was pronounced "Stanton" anyway.

These and other measures have not been wasted on the outside world. Aside from providing other Programs in which to make mistakes, they demonstrate the human frailties of the System, a characteristic with which most can identify and sympathize.

And when the time comes for the System to be called in for an audit on something like the supersonic transport and Lockheed's bankruptcy, the outside world will be quick to forgive and forget.

27

OVERTIMING

THERE ARE A NUMBER of ways of accumulating overtime in Bureaucracy, but working is not one of them. The most common way is to do something different from the many specific duties assigned.

For example: the military is always pushing physical training, the strenuousness and appeal of which varies inversely as the distance from the firing line. So even in the far rear echelons of the Pentagon one finds a directive prescribing: "Physical Training: Military personnel may be excused, consistent with the workload, one afternoon a week for the purpose of participating in an activity associated with physical training." Golf, handball and badminton are included, but mostly golf. Here, then, if one would give the impression of working overtime he must first establish himself a sportsman. Get a locker at the gym; keep a pair of sneakers in the bottom drawer of the desk; talk frequently about little league, bowling scores, and handicaps. Then stay at the desk while others are out working up a sweat. This makes one look deprived; the sacrifice will count as overtime.

I am not the physical type so I greeted with alacrity a Proclamation put out by the Department of Health, Education, and Welfare which warned: "All employees are given advance notice that sometime soon there will be a 'think period.' When a specific announcement is made, all work is stopped for a half hour and employees give thought to some aspect of improving their job. The half hour before lunch has been found to be an excellent time."

Anticipating the proclamation's being put into effect, I attempted to be the first, and at the same time improve upon the idea. I extended the think period to an hour and moved it to the other side of lunch. That way I got in two solid hours of quiet thinking, one of which was overtime. But somehow, after lunch when I was leaning back, feet up on my desk, my eyes closed in concentration, I was unable to convince my superiors that I was thinking.

Another ploy involves making a virtue of necessity. During very cold or very hot or inclement weather, eat lunch at the desk, keeping some office work open so it looks like the lunch is no more than an intrusion on a busy schedule.

Overtiming can be done also through a lack of parking spaces. Many people manage this by leaving for work 20 to 25 minutes early. This guarantees a parking spot and the extra time in the office will be looked upon as overtime especially if one sits bent over the desk striving over work when the regulars come sauntering in at the appointed hour. It's always good to have that settled-in look that one takes on between 10:00 and 11:00—coat off; books and papers scattered around; half-full cup of coffee and slightly rumpled hair.

There is a bonus, too, if the office overlooks the parking lot. Fellowcrats, especially the boss, can't help noticing you as they walk toward the building. Still, with or without the window, you'll know you've scored heavily when the boss asks, "Golly, John. What do you do? Spend the night here?"

Avoiding quitting-time traffic jams can also be converted into overtime. At the day's end, stay at the desk for an extra 20 minutes until the peak slacks off. Extra points will pile up especially if you tell the others, "You all go ahead. I'll check the safes."

Once you've established your overtime points, be careful not to spoil it by making a bid for martyrdom. So when the boss asks why you are working extra, don't grumble about overwork or some fellowcrat not doing his job. Simply say that you had some quick jobs you wanted to get out of the way before the next load hits the fan.

Weekends and holidays can be excellent for overtiming except that the boss won't be there to see you. So some imagination is needed to make the hours pay off. I've seen unpracticed tyrocrats come in, trusting to blind luck that the boss would drop by and see the sacrifice. After a number of aborted runs, one could see the frustration mounting, and feel their almost uncontrollable urge to call the boss at home and shout at him: "Hey! Look at me! I'm here overtime."

Such a ridiculous course is out of the question because there are foolproof ways of doing the shouting without being so obvious. For instance: go to work on Saturday morning and select the file on the subject creating the most havoc at the time. Study it for an obscurity that was overlooked through the week and refresh your memory on some of the figures. Then call the boss: "Good morning, sir. This is John. Sir, I've been going over the specifications on the new runway, and there is a point or two which puzzles me. Could you straighten me out? I sure hate to bother you on a day off, but I thought it was important that we be on top of this before Monday."

Once you have established your presence, have a cup of coffee, read the paper or the book you've brought along and wait around just in case he calls back. Then leave.

Don't use this too often and don't call too early. If you've taken the time to learn the boss' idiosyncrasies you'll know the time and tempo.

An alternative is to leave a note letting him know that you were at the office when you could have been home. It should contain a provocative comment to arouse his anxieties, and some expression of your availability "first thing Monday." In addition to getting you some credit for overtime, it will insure you an audience with the boss, sometimes a good way to begin the week.

When using this tactic, make certain that the date line stands out. For example: don't make it just "3 May." Write it "Saturday, 3 May, 0930", or "Christmas Day, 0800," etc.

There are times when desperate measures are needed. Otherwise one may lapse into Bureaucratic obscurity, a condition more desolate than the Testament's "back side of the desert." So desperate measures are necessary. One fellowcrat was lifted out of such obscurity by using a silhouette of himself bending over his desk. On selected evenings or weekends, he would place it in front of the window so it could be seen from the street. A background light was supplied by a small desk lamp automatically timed to turn on at around 8:00 P.M. and off at 10:00. The effects were impressive and lasting.

While the overtiming methods are surefire, one shouldn't overwork them lest he earn a reputation for being unable to keep up. Finally, before using the telephone or note ploy, check the boss' work patterns carefully. If he's coming in on Saturday mornings and holidays, chances are he needs some points, too. Some mutual disesteem will creep in behind the polite fiction that will be exchanged, for he'll know and you'll know. It will be mutually embarrassing.

28

MANPOWER REDUCTIONS AND PROTECTIVE REORGANIZATIONS

THE TYROCRAT'S BIGGEST headaches are brought on by money-saving drives. Every year or so, powerful forces begin to stir, and like lemmings in their headlong dash to the sea, governments stampede to divest themselves of "excess fat." With cymbals crashing they hail the dawn of a new, lean era.

These "lean era" Programs have a number of descriptive names, ultimately reduced to RIF—Reduction in Forces. Incumbents targeted to be culled are said to be in danger of being "riffed." Positions that are vulnerable are "riffable." (The Program's original title was to have been "Reduction in Expenses, Administration and Manpower"—REAM. However, an alert acronymist concerned with image noted that: " 'He was riffed' sounded much less abrasive than 'He was reamed.' ")

In an acronymic sense, the State Department faced a special problem because their riffing is influenced by flow of gold and balance of payments. To serve these economic factors, many foreign service officers are sent back to the States, having been "balped." Balp is derived from *Bal*ance of *P*ayments— BALP, an awkward sound at best. (One is reminded of the sound made when the plug is pulled on a bathtub.) Flow of Gold was quickly discarded as a base for the new verb when diplocrats realized the effect of a headline saying, "State Department FLOGs Foreign Service Workers."

But whatever the name, the tyrocrat first headaches over the possibility of losing his job. Later as a full blown Bureaucrat, it'll be over his staff being reduced (hence a loss of power and influence), or being on a staff that is to be reduced.

Fears of the first case are groundless. In over a quarter century of Bureaucratting, I've never heard of a new man being discharged who hadn't wanted to be. As for being on a staff that is to be reduced, one can turn to Protective Reorganization. Some methods are described below:

Spacing Method. In the normal course of Bureaucracy, people are always transferring, retiring, resigning, or on detached service, leaving more positions than people. When faced with a RIF, one divides the number of people on hand by the number authorized, subtracts from 100 and submits a report showing the percentage by which the office is already understaffed. A note about how much money was saved to date will strike a proper chord. The most that can happen will be the loss of an empty position or two.

Buffer Method. During good times, outside-world industry hires riffable bodies. When fortunes turn downward, the riffables are discharged in a shower of savings, leaving the original core intact. Bureaucracy shies away from such calloused use of fellowcrats and rifs positions instead. Here detailed justifications are prepared telling why the office should have additional positions authorized. Once approved, they may be left empty or filled with part time workers. When the RIF comes, the buffer positions are sacrificed without effect on the staff.

Fission Method: Once in a while some of the powerful personages find their way into the workaday corridors. When this happens, the first reaction is to wonder where all the people came from because the halls are so crowded. After being elbowed two or three times, they get nervous and words like "overstaffed" crop up. Shortly thereafter there is an order for an "across-the-board" reduction to take place by a certain time.

This headache is serious since the only aspirin available will result in relocation of part of the staff. This is done by creating new organizations in a different location entirely. No power is lost since these branches remain under control of the organizing unit, and are staffed with surplus fellowcrats culled from the older order. Eventually, the parent office's losses are replaced and the new branches begin to become independent entities preparing for and meeting their own RIF problems.

The final step in any Protective Reorganization is the funds-saved report. Compute the amount saved by not having the positions and submit it in an appropriate report. Ultimately it will be used in the effectiveness report as an example of "outstanding managerial ability."

29

WALLS

TODAY, WALLS ARE expected to do more than just surround
the rooms. They are looked upon as ideal places to hang the
charts that show accomplishments past, present, and anticipated. And since walls of Bureaucracy are variegated with preci-
sion graphics, no treatment of the System would be complete
without an explanation of their significance.

The forerunner of all charts is the sign-out board. It began
as a small THINK sign used to cover up a blotch that would
take the customary four months to have repaired. A division
supervisor, upon seeing the sign, directed it be removed because
having to remind Bureaucracy to "THINK" was demeaning.
Faced with more blotches than slogans to cover them, Bureaucracy responded by calling a staff meeting to discuss the problem
and appoint a study group. However, such an assembly was

impossible on the spur of the moment because the staff was out either Coordinating or "overtiming." It didn't take long to realize the advantage that would accrue were there a way to get in touch with the staff when needed. So the sign-out board was invented. Now nearly all offices have one posted near the door and when properly filled in, it shows the Name, Destination, Time Out, and Expected Return, plus a phone number where one can be reached.

Most sign-out boards are works of art being done up in pastels with old English print. They are covered with plastic so the staff can sign out with the grease pencil suspended by a string at the right, then erase the entries using the dirty rag suspended from a similar string on the left.

Now one might imagine that the primary purpose will have been served each time a fellowcrat dutifully makes and clears his entries. But upon close examination, one notes that the string on the grease pencil is not long enough to allow the last man listed to write in all the data required. Likewise, what he can write can't always be erased because the string on the rag isn't long enough either. Moreover, some of the middle and top entries are 4 or 5 days old. Evidently, then, the sign-out board has a more serious purpose. In fact, it is a billboard advertisement used to display, for visitors' benefit, the number of people the chief has working for him, thereby establishing just how much a chief he really is.

One thing led to another, and once the list of workers had been publicly displayed, one had publicly to announce what all the people did. So the Schedule of Events board was invented.

The design varies widely but the more common and efficient is the large formal "calendar" version. Here, a 20" by 40" poster board is laid out in 30 or so blocks so that there is at least one space for each day of the month. Sometimes a 60" by

80″ sheet is used and two months are blocked off. It is also covered with plastic and date-ed, day-ed, and month-ed in grease pencil. Remarks signaling things to be done are greased in, to be erased as rescheduling occurs, and again when it comes to pass.

As a symbol of activity, the Events board can backfire horribly. What could be more embarrassing than 31 or 62 gleaming white, *blank* spaces on a board designed to show how busy the official is. Even with all the meetings, conferences, due dates, and informal activities, satisfying the board's voracious appetite can be a serious problem. That is, unless one knows how to do it.

The secret is to use it as a reminder for personal matters. The only requirement is that care be exercised in the wording. There's nothing so mundane as a reminder saying "Get teeth cleaned" written next to one telling of a coming meeting with the Joint Chiefs of Staff. But if, instead, it reads "Meeting on Operation Gap Filler," it would be perfectly suitable. Likewise, "Get Car Washed" or "Haircut," when written as "Appointment, Transportation Board" and "Products Improvement Seminar," would raise no eyebrows. Nor would "Correspondence Check" for "Mail Letters," "Supply Conference" for "Pick up Groceries," etc. So given the normal pace of Bureaucracy's Projects and Efforts, The Events Board can shout *overwork!* with no more than a little careful wording.

Activities to be done always mean more if displayed in context with the past. Progress Charts, then are used to serve this end. The best ones graph the number of things done over given blocks of time.

Time is labeled across the bottom and quantity up the left side. To show how much was accomplished, a strip of colored tape or an inked-in bar is extended upward from the bottom—

least—toward the top—most, and terminated at the correct value.

Nobody ever really looks closely at these charts; however the observer rarely does more than compare at a glance the amount of covered up with the amount that could be covered. Hence, if there is a lot of white showing, then regardless of the Striving that went into the Efforts, it'll look as though the office has been coasting.

To overcome this, make the value at the top of the chart represent the *average number of things done in a given block of time*. Then when the chart is filled, at least 50 percent of the time, the bars will extend off the chart!

30

GATHERINGS OF BUREAUCRATS

WITH APOLOGIES TO HORACE, "The mountain rumbles and moves and gives birth to a mouse." Bureaucracy, although bigger than a mountain, simply twitches a bit and gives birth to a meeting, and this rumbles and moves.

Gatherings of Bureaucrats are the means the System uses to prepare for the next significant advancement in the evolution of a crisis. Because of the life-pulse nature of meetings, it is essential that the tyrocrat learn the meaning of the throbs. It will soon establish his credentials as a professional attendee and insure that he'll be heard and respected.

Taking a seat in the soft chairs around the conference table, instead of being relegated to the folding traps in the gallery, is an important step. Also significant is understanding that meetings are held under a variety of names. It will avoid confusion and help the attendee adjust his attitude before taking his seat.

For instance, a *meeting* is held locally. It becomes a *conference* when it is held far enough away that one can fly to it. However, a meeting can be a *local conference* if there is a printed agenda, and provisions are made in advance to serve coffee. A conference becomes a *symposium* if nobody has to do anything when it's over, or it doesn't affect the status quo. (This distinction is important. It may be at the root of the communications breakdown which is inhibiting the Paris peace talks on Vietnam. It is obvious that while we are attending a peace *conference*, the North Vietnamese are attending a peace *symposium*.) Also, in a symposium the minutes are often published in advance, handed out, and labeled a Summary of Topics, a convenience which can be touched up and served as the minutes for the meetings and conferences which result from the contacts made at the symposium.

Occasionally one hears about a *seminar*. This is a local symposium, or it may be an exchange of ideas conducted without benefit of a Summary of Topics. Usually, seminars come in a series and are attended by relatively few people.

Gatherings of Bureaucrats, whatever the name, do one or all of the following:

a. Discuss the current status of the Program to insure that there is nothing that will interfere with its successful completion.*

b. Explain how money is going to be spent.

c. Explain why the last amount allocated wasn't enough.

d. Establish a common set of reasons to be advanced when the time comes to explain why something (1) did or did not

---

* Standard terminology when writing the trip justification.

happen; (2) should or should not happen; (3) will or will not happen again.

e. Bring together the vested-interest parties so they can reassure each other that despite all the delays and failures, everything will come out all right in the end.

f. Prove that the costs aren't unreasonable, no matter what the newspapers say.

g. Find ways of complying with a new regulation and still maintain Projects and Tasks just as before.

h. Apportion responsibility.

Gatherings are usually held at times and places of current relevance, making the attendees more worldly. For instance: during Expo 70, scientists from some of the eastern universities engaged in military research set up an international symposium to be held in Tokyo. Locally, such things as the Indianapolis 500, World Series, Pacific Open, and the start of the Colorado ski season make excellent points of relevance about which to form a meeting.

Equally important are the meeting rooms and their appointments. To the tyrocrat, entering the arena for the first time can be a moving experience. The atmosphere is one of soft leather, dark paneling and high ceilings blended into the inconspicuous luxury of old money. The deep-carpeted room is dominated by a long, high-gloss table around which are arranged a discrete number of fully upholstered swivel chairs, plus a high-back one with brass studdings presiding until the chairman comes to occupy it. Note pads, ash trays, pencils or ball point give-aways are placed at attention in front of each chair. Neatly arranged concentrically, but well back from the table are the gallery chairs. (In the meeting rooms such as the one described here, the comfort index decreases with the distance from the table. In the gallery the mood and decor are brought back to

Spartan functionalism through those tricky steel folding chairs so popular at PTA meetings and funeral parlors.) Finally, a well proportioned basic-black-and-pearls secretary with a silver blonde bouffant hair-do breasts-and-legs her way around the room fussing at some last minute straightening, and stimulating everyone into making plans for the evening.

At this point the tyrocrat makes his first real move toward establishing his bona fides. The whole thing right down to the trim-bottomed secretary must be taken coldly for granted. No awe-struck, wide-eyed staring. No overdoing it with disdainful sneers either. One should enter as though going into one's own kitchen for a drink of water.

Clearly, not all meeting rooms are thus appointed—only the ones where super-maestrocrats will be in attendance. Herein lies another lesson: Always contrive to get invited to the meetings having the most rank. (A quick check of announcement rosters will supply the information needed.) In fact, the middle echelon gatherings are held in some small, out-of-the-way room characterized by butt-sprung chairs, low ceilings, no windows, and a sometimes air conditioning unit.

The next step in establishing credentials takes place when the attendees begin the seating ritual. Here I encourage the tyrocrat to hide all traces of modesty and, upon entering the conference room, make directly for a seat at the table. Ignore the gallery completely.

Except for a brief instant at the beginning, there is little likelihood that anybody will ask you to get up. The Good Ole Boy protects you here. Still, there is a possibility that the chairman may lean over and ask you to relinquish your seat, know ing your embarrassment will be covered up in the confusion as other fellowcrats are squirming into place. To avoid such a confrontation, don't let the chairman catch your eye, or even have access to your attention. A good move is to take a stack of papers from your attaché case and study them intently, making margin notes as you go along.

Merely taking the upholstered seat is not enough; you must show that you are worthy of it. This is the final step in establishing yourself as a professional attendee, a man of affairs. One accomplishes this by asking questions. Not just *any* question because you don't want to display any ignorance. On the contrary, make the others display theirs by asking questions that lead them to believe you possess hidden knowledge about the subject. Sound as though you really expect a good answer, don't hurt anybody's feelings, and above all, don't back the fellowcrat questioned into the "I don't know" sequence.

Over the course of years, I have catalogued many questions asked by professional attendees which meet the criteria above. They boil down to five basic requests that can be applied at any time at any conference. The proper inflection is important; the italicized word shows where to place it for the best effect.

a. "I had a different understanding of that. Could you elaborate just a *little?* That might clear me up."

b. "What would be the *impact* if we delayed the start?

c. How is *this* going to affect our *other* programs?"

d. "Why do you want to do it *that* way?"

e. "What's going to be the cost effectiveness of *this* compared to . . . ?"

These piercing inquiries will increase your stature to a level well above your chief competitors, also bent on establishing themselves. The first of the lot is the play-back artist. He also asks questions but they are long and involved and generally repeat something the speaker said earlier. He ends monologue query with "Ya see whatta mean?" Equally boring is the historian who finds it necessary to remind everybody that he is steeped in tenure. Each new proposal is met with "Yes. That's a pretty good approach. It might be worth a try. Although we did something like that about 8 years ago . . . " And so on to remind also that the System is cyclic in nature.

Another is the cloud nine type. He begins by taking issue with a concrete point and pursues the issue through higher and higher levels of abstraction until it is so broad and open ended that nobody present can say definitely what's at stake. He settles it for them by his concluding remark: "You've got some damned good points there. Don't let me talk you out of them. They just need to be thought out a little more."

Another is the dark horse, and he is the biggest nuisance. He is the one who has long since established his credentials but needs reassurance that they are still recognized since the last gathering. Just before the others enter the room, he seeks out the chairman and engages him in conversation calculated to pass on the fact that he has ideas very pertinent to the meeting. Then he enters quietly and takes a seat in the gallery. The confirmation—and his triumph—comes when the chairman, in his opening remarks says, "Good to see you here, Mr. Klinkerton. Why don't you join us at the table. I know you've got some information that's pretty vital to what we're doing." If this happens, the tyrocrat should once more begin to study his papers and perhaps drop a few. Under no circumstances should one offer to relinquish one's chair; nor should one catch the chairman's eye.

The above described are competitors. There are other attendees whose purpose seems only to use up floor time:

a. Dilettante: Works around the edges of the main topic until he can seize on a lead which will steer the discussion around to something he's familiar with.

b. The court jester: Although an attendee, he's not really

well enough grounded to make any constructive comments. When cornered he will joke his way through an answer. Once aroused, he continues to wise-crack through the rest of the day to establish good will, then disappears for the rest of the conference.

c. The sleeper: Just along for the ride. Sits far back in the gallery and sleeps to recover from the previous night's excesses, and prepare for the evening to come.

d. The phantom conferee: Unseen but never, never unheard, this participant is best recognized through the following fictitious but not improbable briefing:

"All right gentlemen. Take your places, please, and we'll get started. We've got a busy day today as the schedule shows. To begin with, there are two big meetings set up. So, Joe, you take the heating duct rattler up to the third floor so it will be in place in the morning. Start it going about 0945. That will take care of the conference in 312. Charlie. Get the push cart with the steel wheels. You know the one. It has the flat spot on the right front. Load it with some empty buckets and some sheets of scrap galvanized and roll it up and down the east wing just outside 475B. Make your first pass at 1000 hours sharp. Mike. How about you taking the small sledgehammer and tap around under the floor below the main auditorium.

"Now. I need somebody to work on the projector in 734 for tomorrow afternoon. The last time it was used it went all the way through the film without breaking down or burning a bulb. Besides, the screen was in place *before* the meeting started. No excuse for that! Chuck. Take care of it.

"Jackson. 424—the new meeting room. They're opening tomorrow. Run up there and gather up all the chalk that's long enough to use. Check the drawers and all for any long pieces somebody might have hidden away. On your way, take some of

155

the paper towels out of the men's room next to 312. When I checked it there was enough in the dispenser to last all day. I want it to run out about 1150 when the meeting breaks for lunch.

"OK. That's it. You have your orders! Move out!"

Irrespective of participants, real or phantom, conferences, symposia, meetings and other gatherings that convene regularly eventually evolve into committees. If these meet regularly in the same place, they become standing committees where each member has his own plush chair, thus giving lie to the name. Committees appoint subcommittees which in turn appoint study groups. Progress thereafter is made in specific steps. (Please return now to step 1, page 33, and review the Program Cycle, if necessary.)

31

CLERKDOM

BUREAUCRACY AND THE Outside World, i.e., the doer and the done for, come together at the *clerk*.

And clerks are omnipresent.

There are license tag clerks who inform you that they accept only cash or a money order; there are supply clerks who tell you that the requisition should have been signed by somebody else; the tax clerk tells you where to sit while you wait for help on the 1040; the clerk outside the traffic court authoritatively checks off your name as she tells you curtly that the judge will be an hour late; the voucher clerk disallows the 15 percent tip because she deems it excessive; and the appointment clerk closes the calendar and window just as your turn comes; and on and on ad infinitum.

Together, these fellowcrats form a System within the System—Clerkdom. Their organization, albeit a de facto one, has three tenets which, if followed, automatically make one a member, clerkdom being more a state of mind than a job. An honest-to-God, dyed-in-the-spirit clerk must have an infinite capacity to inconvenience infinitely. He must have an unsurpassed knowledge of regulations. And he must look upon everybody not in his immediate sphere—in or out of Bureaucracy—as the Outside World. Armed with these, the most insignificant clerk in the Bureau is quite at home jerking the chair from under even those who sit in the seats of the mighty.

And unless one understands the plight of clerkdom, one is apt to think the rank and file get a sadistic pleasure out of doing just that. The difficulty is this, though: while clerks have the might and power of the System *behind* them, they have nothing at all out in front. Being thus exposed, they are the first to feel the undiffused wrath of those incensed at having to take time out to appear before Bureaucracy and do its bidding. So the clerks must maintain a posture of constant defense so well-developed that sometimes they may *seem* to be offensive. The shield is made up in part of being icily polite, coldly aloof, completely in command, 100 percent right 100 percent of the time even if they are wrong, and never forgetting for an instant that they are the slots into which the System's inputs are first dropped. A failure in any one of these would lead the done fors to take advantage of the System and shatter the conformity upon which its machinery depends.

Clerks understand the cyclic nature of the System and know that all who come before it must come again, and so should be taught their lesson the first time. There is no time to explain repeatedly the effects of non-compliance, so the shock treatment is used. This gives the impression that the clerks are being mean as hell whereas they are really helping you avoid the little mistakes the next time around. It's like the old mule-skinner who used to hit his mule between the eyes with a two-by-four when he was trying to train him. Told he'd get more through kindness, the grizzled old man replied, "Yep. I know it. But I got to get his attention first."

Therefore, when one is told by the clerk that the wrong blocks were left blank; entries are illegible; pen, not pencil is to be used or vice versa; black ink, not blue is required; vice versa; 3 more copies are needed; or when an obscure regulation is dusted off to stop your arguments and squish your request; and it's all done in such a way that you are brought to instant rage, the clerk is not being officious or flaunting his authority. He's just getting your attention.

One should swallow the indignation and rage. Show that the two-by-four found its mark. Upon regaining composure, ask him, or even plead with him a little, to use his experience and know-how to assist you in avoiding any more inconvenience. If you are properly contrite, he'll do just that. The practiced clerk will be quick to catch your acknowledgement of his plight, and as a reward for your understanding, will do as you request if at all possible. However, it will be done with considerable viscosity, this to notify you that you are indeed receiving a rarely granted favor.

There are compensations in this for clerkdom, too. By the time it is all over, he will have made an ally and champion. It's rare that one can win a victory over clerkdom, so there is bound to be some bragging. In the process the victor will mention the "good ole boy" who helped him over the hurdles.

But what about the defendant who is too pride-bound to pay a little homage? The question is best answered by the clerk who, with knowing, narrow-eyed menace said: "All I have to do is change a person's extension every other day, delay the re-routing of correspondence, fail to press for a prompt repair or replacement of a broken typewriter, assign a 'dud' to the secretarial pool, forget to authorize secretarial overtime, limit the grade of the secretarial positions, place a grant package at the bottom of the pile rather than on top—and that person is a walking corpse."

And with this revelation, we lay to rest once and for all the canard that often the only signs of life to be detected in some Federal employees is the spasmodic clutching that occurs when their pay check is waved before them. They are not shiftless and lazy. They are the corpses of clerkdom.

32

ETC.

WASHINGTON IN FEBRUARY is dreary. Nonetheless, one can't simply stay home from work because the day is cold and leaden. At least not all the time. The System must have some loyalties paid to it, after all. Obedient, then, to whatever instinct it is that makes me a skilled and practicing Bureaucrat, I plod my way down the front steps to the car. Sweeping the snow from the windshield while I wait for the engine to warm up, I dream of retirement and sunshine.

The route to work is etched into my habits and there's plenty of time to think about things other than where the next turn-off will be. By the time I arrive, I decide that for a text on Bureaucracy, this is a good note upon which to close.

Clearly, there is more to be covered before the tyrocrat has in his possession the keys to the soft, deep carpets and the desks with the Corinthian columns. For example: nothing has been said of the *Crash Program*, once wrongly equated to "getting

161

nine women pregnant so you can have a baby in one month." Omitted, too, is any mention of the *Secretaries*, the real power behind the office because they type the final papers on one's PET Project according to past homages and present whims. And, they type the travel vouchers. Then there are the *Briefings*, and how they can be turned into a formal method of non-communication to save a Program. Even such a mundane subject as *getting repairs and repainting done* should be treated because it is a training ground for professional negotiators slated to take over in the next generation of disarmament talks. The correct use of the *Telephone* as a device that admits one to places at times when a personal visit will not, *Desk Decorating, The Expert, Organization Naming, Security Classifications*, all these and more, must be mastered if one is to get the most out of the System.

But these are complex and properly belong in another text. In the meantime, tyrocrats must learn the hard way.

EPILOGUE

I'D LIKE TO CLOSE this text as I would a conference, i.e., with a word of admonition by way of saying thanks for your attendance. So I'll repeat the advice I gave a young second lieutenant 20-odd years ago, and who, incidentally, retired as a captain after peaking out his career as a Personnel Affairs Officer and Guidance Counselor to a squadron of National Guard fighter pilots. Upon asking me how to get ahead, I recited to him the motto which still hangs well-framed and conspicuously in the prime space above my desk and between the Projects Status Board and a graph I keep that displays the overtime I've accrued. It reminds that—

Pressed for simultaneous non-coordinated decisions by pragmatic opportunists, it is best not to stampede into espousing contingency measures. Instead, peripherize your view of the motives and assess the repercussions through calling a meeting. Out of it will come the unpolarized, extramarginal consensus needed to make the decision comfortable. Failing this, allocate the effort among knowledgeable personnel thereby availing oneself to their expertise, and at the same time, optimizing distribution of responsibility thus dulling the teeth of gnawing doubt.

—The Finalization—

GLOSSARY

ACRONYMIZING: Art of making words by combining the first one or two letters of a group of words.

BACKGROUND: Saving everything in writing to a) prove that you *did* contribute to a successful program; or b) prove that you did *not* contribute to an unsuccessful one.

B-DAY: Bureaucracy Day; 13 November 1982; date on which everyone in United States will be a Bureaucrat.

BS: The Old Bureaucratic System; often referred to as "The ole BS."

BUARCHY: Ultimate state of Bureaucracy wherein those who are served by the System will be caused more trouble by not complying with the program than if they did; inevitable predecessor to anarchy.

BUD NIPPING: In rendering a Presentation, the group is asked to withhold its questions until the talk is finished. The hope is that the question will be forgotten by then.

COB: Corridors of Bureaucracy.

CONFERENCE: Gathering of Bureaucrats that is held far enough away that one must fly to it.

COORDINATION: Insurance that everyone will be involved at every step of the Program Cycle.

COUNTERSINKING: Elaborating on well-established words to insure clarification.

FEAR OF UNFORESEEN DISASTER (FUD): Fear of being proved grotesquely wrong after a Program has been formally accepted into the System; also known as "the open-fly syndrome."

FELLOWCRAT: Fellow Bureaucrat.

FINALIZE: To complete, to finish, to end.

FLOOD-GATE METHOD: Manner of responding to a question at end of a Presentation; if you have no answer, answer a related one at great length.

FORMEES: Those who receive and/or must fill out forms.

FORMSMANSHIP: Use of blank spaces and questions to get formees to pay serious attention to filling out the answers.

FORMSMEN: Those who devote full time to looking after forms.

FOSP: Furniture, Office Space, and People; ordering FOSP is part of the function of the planning staff in the Program Cycle.

GOB: "Good Ole Boy;" a highly respected subclassification of Bureaucrat.

GOVERNMENT GREEN PAINT: A noxious shade of green seen in government offices and frequently in hospitals and schools.

HERNIOLOGY: Hernia-giving terminology.

HONOR GUARD PHRASES: Certain stylized groups of words that are used to overcome the handicaps imposed by the outside world's lack of linguistic versatility.

LANCE AND WINDMILL SYNDROME: Rearrangement of furniture and cleaning of offices to "clear the head."

LOCAL CONFERENCE: A conference that is held locally but has a printed agenda and at which coffee is served.

MAESTROCRAT: Practicing, experienced Bureaucrat.

MEETING: Gathering of Bureaucrats that is held locally.

MEGABUCK: Basic counting unit of MUD; the million.

MONEY OF UNSPECIFIED DENOMINATION (MUD): Legal tender used for Bureaucratting.

NEGATIVE ATTITUDE: That which causes one to frequently use or misuse the syllable "no." Also referred to as the Spectre of Negativism.

NEOLOGIZING: Old words are given new life through changing their spelling, pronunciation, or both.

NON-CONFORMITY: Making an exception to a Bureaucratic rule.

OJT: On-the-job training.

OPERATION MOOSE: "Move Everybody Out Of Saigon Earliest"; plan to stop the problem of gold flow in Vietnam.

OPT: Organized Processing Techniques; known ultimately as The System.

OVERTIME: To do something different from the many specific duties assigned.

OWP: Outside World People; those who are not Bureaucrats.

PEBGBGAS: People Employed Because Government Buys Goods and Services.

PET: Principle of Equal Treatment; as in PET Project, i.e., Bureaucracy does not play favorites and believes in complete equality.

PRINCIPLE OF AMORPHISM: Issuing Proclamations using the right blend of impersonalisms.

PROTECTIVE REORGANIZATION: Way of preventing a staff reduction.

PROTECTIVE VOCABULARY: Bureaucratese.

REDUCTION IN FORCES (RIF): The act of firing, of terminating employment; most commonly a lessening in staff by not replacing retiring persons or filling empty staff positions.

REPORTS: Vary in size from 20-300 pages; either go into a Study or come out of one; must not look too expensive.

RITUAL OF PRESENTATION (ROP): Ceremonial features of award-giving and -receiving.

SEMINAR: Local symposium; usually a series of Bureaucrat-gatherings, attended by few people.

SHILL METHOD: Preparing a question to be asked by a fellowcrat at the end of a Presentation, thus forestalling more, perhaps embarrassing, questions.

SNOWJOB: Sympathy, Neighborliness, Objectivity, Willingness, Joviality, Open-mindedness, Benignity; characteristics Bureaucrats must possess to be considered a GOB.

SOB: Sons of Bureaucracy.

STUDIES: Commonly a written piece of from 350-500 pages; may come in sets of numerous volumes; must contain the following: a) table of contents, b) summary of preceding volumes, c) glossary of terms, d) individual chapters or sections, each with a summary and list of definitions, e) acknowledgements, f) bibliography, g) exhibits, h) appendix, i) annex, j) index.

STUDY GROUP: The original step in the Program Cycle.

SYMPOSIUM: A conference after which nobody has to do anything.

THREE-PLY WEIGHT FACTORS: Verbal symbols that add profundity to light weight communications.

THOU (or K): Unit below Megabuck in computing MUD.

TYROCRAT: Novice Bureaucrat.

UNIVERSAL RESPONSE: Art of phrasing an answer so that it can be used to respond to any question one might be asked in any subject at any time.

WATT: Welcome and Timely Treatise (i.e., this text).